Method of Measurement of Construction Works

Seventh Edition

SI & Imperial Version

by
Geoffrey A.S. Hadley, PQS(F)
Author and Editor

Method of Measurement of Construction Works, 7th edition, 2000
ISBN # 1-896606-28-8
Reprinted 2004
(ISBN # 1-896606-00-8, 6th edition, 1993)

Contents

PREFACE TO THE SEVENTH EDITION

This edition of the Method of Measurement of Construction Works continues the format of the sixth edition, published in 1993. This revision has been necessitated in order to relate to the 1995 edition of "MasterFormat", the Master List of Numbers and Titles for the Construction Industry. Acknowledgment is made to Construction Specifications Canada (CSC) and to The Construction Specifications Institute (USA) (CSI) for permission to use the "Numbers" and "Titles" from "MasterFormat". The Method of Measurement is suitable for either manual or computerized operations.

The Method of Measurement includes a section entitled "General Rules", which contains basic instruction for measuring and for descriptions, and which applies to all 16 Divisions. Within each Division the predominant form of measurement for that Division is given in the introductory paragraphs; subsequent paragraphs are detailed in the order of "MasterFormat".

The Method of Measurement of Construction Works is published by the Canadian Institute of Quantity Surveyors. The Institute was founded on 12 February 1959, and is the governing body for 1,200 quantity surveyors and construction estimators in Canada, who each belong to a Provincial Association affiliated to the Institute. Provincial Associations are presently established in Alberta, British Columbia, Newfoundland and Labrador, Nova Scotia, Ontario and Quebec.

The invaluable assistance of Janette Wheeler of Victoria, B.C., who provided a gratuitous typing service, is gratefully acknowledged.

Geoffrey A. S. Hadley, PQS

Author and Editor

January 2000

With this reprinting of The Method of Measurement of Construction Works, we have attempted to reduce wasteful repetition by combining those portions of this publication that are, to all intents and purposes, the same for both metric and imperial versions.

INTRODUCTION

1. Building works are measured for many reasons, including estimating, ordering and confirming the quantities of materials in place. This "Method of Measurement of Construction Works" provides a uniform basis for measurement.

MEASUREMENTS

1. The quantities of work shall always be accurately measured. Work shall be measured net as fixed in position and each measurement shall be taken to the nearest 10 mm (i.e. 5 mm and over shall be regarded as 10 mm and less than 5 mm shall be disregarded). For Imperial measurement, work shall be measured net as fixed in position and each measurement shall be taken to the nearest 1inch (i.e. ½ inch and over shall be regarded as 1 inch and less than ½ inch shall be disregarded). (See special rules in Division 15 for measuring ductwork). This rule shall not apply to any dimensions stated in descriptions. Where an item, by its nature, requires laps, tongues, grooves, etc., this shall be stated in the description; the amount of lap shall be stated but additional measurement for such laps will not be made unless otherwise described herein.

2. Dependent upon the type of work, measurements will be lineal, square, cubic, enumerated or by weight. Wherever applicable, cross-sectional dimensions shall be given in the description of items measured lineal, thicknesses shall be given in the description of items measured square, and all dimensions shall be given in the description of items enumerated. The cross-sectional dimensions of weighted metal items shall be given.

3. Where minimum deduction of voids are dealt with in this document they shall refer only to openings which are within the boundaries of measured areas. Openings, which are at the boundaries of measured areas, shall always be the subject of deduction irrespective of size.

4. Quantities shall be measured to the nearest whole unit.

DESCRIPTIONS

1. The order of stating dimensions in descriptions shall be consistent and generally in the sequence of length, width and height. Where that sequence is not appropriate, or where ambiguity could arise, the dimensions shall be specifically identified.

DESCRIPTIONS (Continued)

2. Unless otherwise specifically stated in the description, the following shall be deemed to be included with all items:
   1. Labour and all associated costs
   2. Materials and all associated costs
   3. Placing or installing materials in position
   4. Equipment and all associated costs
   5. Waste on materials
   6. Square cutting

3. Where preferred, the supply of a material, and the placing or installing of the material, may be measured as two separate items.

4. Raking cutting, circular cutting, and scribing of rigid materials shall be measured in metres. For Imperial measurement, raking cutting, circular cutting, and scribing of rigid materials shall be measured in feet.

5. Dependent upon the purpose to which the quantities are to be used, their description may be in detail, or abbreviated. If abbreviated, the measurer must ensure that the descriptions are sufficiently identified so that there is no possibility of ambiguity in the mind of the end user. The end use of the item shall always be separately identified in the description, e.g. in "Division 3 - Concrete", concrete shall be separately described as in foundations, walls, suspended slabs, etc; in "Division 6 - Wood and Plastics", separate items shall be given for joists, purlins, rafters, etc. Mitres, ends, etc., where applicable, are deemed to be included in the main measurement of the item.

6. Where appropriate, reference may be made to proprietary items, using the manufacturer's reference. Any alternative finishing treatments shall be clearly identified.

7. In the case of complex items, a description may be supported by a sketch, or a reference to an appropriate drawing.

8. The background to which an item is installed shall be stated.

9. Circular work shall be given separately; the term "circular" shall be deemed to include any form of curve. Circular work shall be described as circular on plan, circular on elevation, or circular on plan and elevation.

DESCRIPTIONS (Continued)

10. This "Method of Measurement" has been presented, as far as possible, within the "MasterFormat" system. "MasterFormat" is a "Master List of Titles and Numbers for the Construction Industry", and is published by Construction Specifications Canada (CSC), and The Construction Specification Institute (US) (CSI). The "MasterFormat" numbers have been quoted extensively in this "Method of Measurement" for possible use in computer-aided measurements. Not all items which are listed in "MasterFormat" are included in this "Method of Measurement"; the principles of measurement set out herein shall apply to similar items contained in "MasterFormat" but not referred to in this document.

WORK IN SPECIAL CONDITIONS

1. Alterations and repair work in existing buildings shall be so described. Handling materials and getting them in or out of such buildings shall be deemed to be included with the items. Labour on existing work shall be so described. Work in underpinning shall be so described.

2. Work carried out in or under water shall be so described stating whether lake, canal, river or sea water and, where applicable, the mean spring levels of high and low water.

3. Work carried out in compressed air shall be so described stating the pressure and the method of entry and exit.

TEMPORARY WORKS

1. Temporary works shall not be measured, unless described in this "Method of Measurement", e.g. formwork, or are an owner-designed item specifically required by the Contract.

Method of Measurement of Construction Works

Seventh Edition

MasterFormat

Method of Measurement of Construction Works

Seventh Edition

SI Version

GENERALLY

1. The section "General Rules" is to be read in conjunction with this Division.

2. The various classifications within the scope of this Division shall be measured and priced as "Items", (unless a specific mode of measurement is recommended).

01100 - SUMMARY

1. 01100 - Summary of work

   1. Personnel

      Include all managerial, technical and administrative personnel (such as project manager, superintendent, foreman, engineer, timekeeper, first-aid attendant, etc.) necessary to ensure the efficient operation of the project, together with attendant expenses.

   2. Mobilization

      Include all costs incurred for moving onto the site, mobilization and set-up; and moving out at completion of project.

   3. Rental of adjacent property

      Include the rental of adjacent property, including restoration of any damage.

   4. Rental of parking meters, sidewalks and land

      Include all charges in connection with fees and licences for rental of parking meters, sidewalks and land.

   5. Camp

      Include the cost of establishing a camp for the workforce, maintenance, provisions and supplies, and removing at completion of the project.

   6. Bonds

      Include the cost of Bid, Performance, Labour and Material Payment and Guarantee Bonds, Certified Cheques and Securities, as specified.

01100 - SUMMARY (Continued)

1.   01100 - Summary of work (Continued)

   7.   Insurances

   Include the cost of all insurances specified for the project, including Demolition, All Risk and Public Liability.

   8.   Finances

   Include the cost of any interim financing

01300 - ADMINISTRATIVE REQUIREMENTS

1.   01300 - Project Management and Coordination

   1.   Head office travel

   Include all expenses incurred by supervisory personnel on regular visits to the site.

2.   01330 - Submittal procedures

   1.   Construction photographs

   Include the cost of site photographs if required by the Specification.

01400 - QUALITY REQUIREMENTS

1.   01410 - Regulatory requirements

   1.   Permanent utility connections

   Include any charges for the permanent connection of hydro, water, gas, sanitary and storm sewers, if not included in another Division.

   2.   Travel expenses

   Include time lost in travel to and from site, travel allowances payable under trade agreements, and allowances for board and lodging.

01400 - QUALITY REQUIREMENTS (Continued)

1. 01410 - Regulatory requirements (Continued)

    3. Miscellaneous permits

        Include all miscellaneous permits pertaining to the project, including utility inspection charges, sidewalk and road repairs, and damage deposits.

    4. Premium time

        Include the cost of premium time to meet schedule requirements stipulated in the tender documents.

    5. Permits

        Include the cost of the Building Permit, Development Permit and Development Cost Charges.

    6. Warranty programs

        Include the cost of complying with all required warranty programs.

    7. Labour rate increase

        Include all labour rate increases that may occur during the duration of the project.

    8. Payroll levies

        Include all payment levies; e.g. holiday pay, U.I.C., C.P.P., union dues, apprenticeship training funds and the like, if not included in the labour rates used for pricing.

    9. Sales taxes

        Include all applicable Provincial Sales Taxes and Federal dues.

    10. Goods and Services Tax

        Include the Goods and Services Tax, noting any special exemptions or reductions to the current tax rate.

01400 - QUALITY REQUIREMENTS (Continued)

2.   01450 - Quality control

1.   Material testing

Include the cost of testing concrete, gravel or backfill compaction, asphalt and any other testing required by the Specification, unless paid for by the Owner.

01500 - TEMPORARY FACILITIES AND CONTROL

1.   Provide, erect, operate, maintain and remove temporary facilities and controls for use on site during construction, including all necessary operators, labour and attendance, fuel, maintenance, repairs, spare parts, moving to and from site, loading and unloading, charges and rentals.

2.   01510 - Temporary utilities

1.   Electricity
2.   Fire protection
3.   Fuel oil
4.   Heating, cooling and ventilating
5.   Lighting
6.   Natural gas
7.   Telephone
8.   Water
9.   Sewers

3.   01520 - Construction facilities

Include furniture, office equipment, telephone, facsimile machine and supplies.

1.   Field offices and sheds
2.   First aid
3.   Sanitary facilities
4.   Fire protection including portable fire extinguishers and fire hoses

4.   01530 - Temporary construction

1.   Bridges
2.   Decking
3.   Ramps

01500 - TEMPORARY FACILITIES AND CONTROL (Continued)

5.   01540 - Temporary construction aids

1.   Construction elevators, hoists and cranes (include bases)
2.   Scaffolding and platforms
3.   Swing staging
4.   Wind bracing (if not included elsewhere in the Specification)
5.   Stairs and ladders
6.   Garbage and disposal chutes
7.   Pumping and other equipment (if not priced under trade operations)
8.   Small tools
9.   Winter protection (include tarpaulins, heaters, temporary enclosures, insulation mats, heated concrete, snow and ice removal)

6.   01550 - Vehicular access and parking

1.   Access roads (measurements shall be in metres)
2.   Parking and storage areas (measurements shall be in square metres)
3.   Traffic control

7.   01560 - Temporary barriers and enclosures

Provide for protection of occupants, the general public or existing spaces, including:

1.   Barricades
2.   Dust barriers and temporary partitions
3.   Fences
4.   Protective walkways (include lighting)
5.   Tree and plant protection
6.   Planking for the protection of trenches and pits (include   safety lamps and warning signs)
7.   Shoring/underpinning (unless included in other Divisions as part of the permanent work)
8.   Railings to perimeters of floors and roofs and at openings as required to meet Workers Compensation Board regulations

Include painting where required. Measurements shall be in metres, square metres, or enumerated as appropriate.

01500 - TEMPORARY FACILITIES AND CONTROL (Continued)

8.   01570 - Temporary controls

    1.   Temporary site drainage, including pumping any temporary ditches, sumps, catch-basins and shoring the face of excavations.
    2.   Watchman or security services
    3.   Flagman or signalman

9.   01580 - Project identification

    1.   Project signs

01700 - EXECUTION REQUIREMENTS

1.   01720 - Field engineering

    1.   Providing labour, materials and instruments for the proper layout out of the works.

    2.   Include for the services and fees of a professional land surveyor.

2.   01740 - Cleaning

    1.   Final cleaning

    Include removing all temporary or protective coverings; washing and final polishing of all windows and other glass surfaces including the inside of unsealed double glazing units, floor and wall tiles, sheet goods and the like; vacuuming carpets; cleaning, oiling and adjusting hardware. Measurements may be in square metres, or as an item.

    2.   Progress cleaning

    3.   Site maintenance

    Include keeping the site and building free from all rubbish, provision of disposal container and dumping charges.

3.   01760 - Protecting installed construction

    Provide and maintain temporary coverings to floors and finished work and remove on completion. Measurements shall be in square metres.

01800 - FACILITY OPERATION

1. 01830 - Operation and maintenance

    1. Maintenance

        Include the cost of any required maintenance of the building, equipment and systems and the site development work after installation and during subsequent construction.

        Where specifically required, include the cost of any required maintenance after substantial completion.

GENERALLY

1. The section "General Rules" is to be read in conjunction with this Division.

02100 - SITE REMEDIATION

1. Site remediation shall be measured in the following categories:

    02105 - Chemical sampling and analysis
    02110 - Excavation, removal and handling of hazardous material
    02115 - Underground storage tank removal
    02120 - Off-site transportation and disposal
    02130 - Site decontamination
    02150 - Hazardous waste recovery processes
    02160 - Physical treatment
    02170 - Chemical treatment
    02180 - Thermal processes
    02190 - Biological processes

2. 02105 - Chemical sampling and analysis shall be stated as an item.

3. 02110 - Hazardous material

    1. The removal of hazardous material, such as asbestos, requires the preparation of the work area, including providing a negative air pressure and the provision of a decontamination unit. The hazardous material may be covered by a finish material, such as drywall, or ceiling tile, which itself will be contaminated, and must be removed prior to removing the hazardous material.

    2. Temporary floor covering, and taping and sealing door and window openings, shall each be measured separately in square metres. The provision of an air pump, including the replacement of filters, shall be enumerated. The setting up, maintenance and removal of a decontamination unit shall be enumerated.

    3. The removal of the covering material shall be measured in square metres.

    4. The removal of hazardous material shall be measured as follows:

        1. From floors, walls and ceilings - in square metres
        2. From pipes - in metres
        3. From boilers, and other items of equipment - enumerated.

02100 - SITE REMEDIATION (Continued)

5. The disposal of hazardous material and contaminated waste shall be given as an item.

4. 02120 - Underground storage tank removal shall be enumerated.

5. 02130 - Site decontamination shall be measured in square metres.

6. 02160 - 02190 - Soil decontamination shall be measured in cubic metres.

02200 - SITE PREPARATION

1. Site preparation shall be measured in the following categories;

    02220 - Site demolition
    02230 - Site clearing
    02240 - Dewatering
    02250 - Shoring and underpinning
    02260 - Excavation support and protection

2. 02220 - Site demolition

    1. General principles

        1. Any assumptions made in the preparation of the measurement shall be so stated.

        2. Material to be salvaged, either for reuse or for handing over to the Owner, shall be so described.

        3. General protection shall not be measured. Special protection, where specified, either on a permanent or temporary basis, shall be measured in accordance with the relevant Divisions of this Method of Measurement.

        4. The removal of demolished items from site, and their final disposal shall be measured separately.

        5. Special insurance requirements shall be stated in Division 1.

02200 - SITE PREPARATION (Continued)

2.   02220 - Site demolition (Continued)

2.   Building demolition

1.   Structures to be completely demolished shall be enumerated and described in general terms, giving the type of structure and building systems, and the overall dimensions.

3.   Selective demolition

1.   Parts of structures to be demolished shall be measured in detail within this Section. No deductions shall be made from the measurements of openings for doors, windows, skylights and the like.

2.   Temporary shoring, where required, shall be stated with the item of demolition.

3.   Work relating to making good shall be measured in accordance with the relevant Divisions of this Method of Measurement.

4.   Demolition of concrete foundations, columns, beams, and staircases shall be measured in cubic metres and described as reinforced or unreinforced.

5.   Demolition of roads, floors, walls and roofs shall be measured in square metres. Applied finishings shall be described.

6.   Demolition of structural steel columns, beams, joists, etc. shall each be separately enumerated.

7.   Demolition of doors, windows, millwork, specialties, etc. shall be enumerated.

8.   Demolition of suspended ceilings shall be measured in square metres.

9.   Cutting or enlarging openings in walls, floors and roofs shall be enumerated.

10.   Demolition of conveying systems and mechanical and electrical services shall be measured in the same units used for installation, as described in the relevant Divisions in this Method of Measurement.

02200 - SITE PREPARATION (Continued)

2. 02220 - Site demolition (Continued)

   3. Selective demolition (Continued)

      11. Disconnecting and capping services and utilities shall be enumerated.

3. 02230 - Site clearing

   1. An item of "Site clearing" shall be measured in square metres to cover the removal of shrubs, trees (not exceeding 300 mm girth) and other vegetable matter.

   2. Trees to be removed shall be enumerated and grouped according to size (measured 1.50 m above ground level) as follows:

      Exceeding 300 mm but not exceeding 900 mm girth
      Exceeding 900 mm but not exceeding 1 800 mm girth
      Exceeding 1 800 mm but not exceeding 2 700 mm girth

      The item shall be deemed to include cutting down, grubbing up roots and burning or removing material from site.

   3. Stripping and disposal of top soil (either off site or stored on site for later reuse in landscaping) shall be measured ("bank measure") in cubic metres.

   4. The demolition of fences, walls and the like shall be measured in metres; the items shall be deemed to include the removal of foundations and disposal off site.

4. 02240 - Dewatering

   1. The removal of subsurface water for preparation of foundations, pipe bedding and other work shall be given as an item.

5. 02250 - Shoring and underpinning

   1. When shoring is specifically ordered, it shall be measured in square metres to both sides of trenches and to the faces of other excavations.

   2. The length of the wall to be supported in underpinning shall be measured in metres. Details of the wall shall include the height, number of floors and type of foundation.

02200 - SITE PREPARATION (Continued)

6.   02260 - Excavation support and protection

   1.   Soil and rock anchors shall be enumerated in this category.

02300 - EARTHWORK

1.   General principles

   1.   Earthwork shall be measured in the following categories:

      02310 - Grading
      02315 - Excavation and fill
      02335 - Subgrade and roadbed
      02340 - Soil stabilization
      02370 - Erosion and sedimentation control

   2.   Earthwork shall be measured in cubic metres unless otherwise stated.

   3.   Excavation and fill shall be measured "bank measure".

   4.   The type of material to be excavated shall be stated. Any restrictions on blasting, where the excavation is in rock, shale or hardpan, shall be stated.

   5.   Allowances for working space for temporary shoring, the erection and removal of formwork, the application of waterproofing or the laying of pipes shall be as follows:

      1.   To footing - 150 mm from face of footing or 600 mm from face of wall above, whichever is greater.

      2.   To trench and face of mass excavation - 600 mm from face of wall or 150 mm from face of footing below, whichever is greater.

      3.   To trenches for pipes not exceeding 300 mm in diameter plus 300 mm on each side of the pipe.

      4.   To trenches for pipes exceeding 300 mm in diameter plus 600 mm on each side of the pipe.

      Where special circumstances require the provision of more working space than indicated above, the assumed dimensions of the working space shall be stated.

02300 - EARTHWORK (Continued)

1. General principles (Continued)

    5. (Continued)

        Alternatively, if customary in the particular location, working space shall not be measured and this shall be so stated.

    6. Unless permanent shoring is measured, additional excavation shall be measured to permit the following angles of repose:

Rock, shale and hardpan	nil
Stiff clay	4:1
Clay	3:1
Earth	2:1
Sand	1:1

    7. Temporary shoring of excavation shall not be measured. Permanent shoring or other form of protection shall be measured in square metres to all faces to be upheld.

    8. All excavation items shall be deemed to include dumping on site in spoil heaps. An item shall be measured for disposal off site for material surplus to requirements. Fill from borrow pits on site, and imported fill, shall be measured separately.

2. 02310 - Grading

    1. Grading shall be measured in square metres.

3. 02315 - Excavation and fill

    1. Excavating, mass fill and backfill shall be classified as follows:

        1. Bulk work to reduce or make up levels
        2. Basements
        3. Trenches
        4. Column bases and pits
        5. Ducts and miscellaneous
        6. Shafts, manholes and wells
        7. Trenches for the mechanical and electrical trades
        8. Work required to be performed by hand or by some other specified means.

02300 - EARTHWORK (Continued)

3. 02315 - Excavation and fill (Continued)

    2. Trimming and grading bottoms or sides of excavation shall not be measured unless they are to be used as formwork.

4. 02335 - Subgrade and roadbed

    1. Preparation of subgrades and roadbeds shall be measured in square metres.

5. 02340 - Soil stabilization

    1. Soil stabilization shall be measured in square metres.

6. 02370 - Erosion and sedimentary control

    1. Paving, blankets and mats shall be measured in square metres.

    2. Gabions, riprap and the like shall be measured in cubic metres.

    3. Water course and slope erosion protection shall be measured in metres.

02400 - TUNNELING, BORING AND JACKING

1. Tunnel excavation etc. shall be measured in this category. The general principles and method of measurement contained in other clauses in this Division shall apply.

02450 - FOUNDATION AND LOAD-BEARING ELEMENTS

1. General principles

    1. Foundation and load-bearing elements shall be measured in the following categories:

        02455 - Driven piles
        02465 - Bored piles
        02475 - Caissons
        02490 - Anchors

    2. Piles shall be measured in metres, from tip to cut-off level, unless otherwise stated.

02450 - FOUNDATION AND LOAD-BEARING ELEMENTS (Continued)

1. General principles (Continued)

    3. All available information relating to the site and sub-surface conditions shall be given with the measurements of piling.

    4. Restrictions relating to the level from which piling may be driven shall be stated.

    5. Piling which is to be carried out in water or under any limiting conditions relating to access or methods shall be measured separately, stating the restrictions.

    6. The cost of all record keeping shall be included in the piling rate.

    7. Anchors shall be enumerated.

2. 02455 - Driven piles

    1. Piling shall be classified as follows:

        1. Cast-in-place concrete piles
        2. Composite piles
        3. Concrete displacement piles
        4. Concrete filled steel piles
        5. Precast concrete piles
        6. Prestressed concrete piles
        7. Sheet piles
        8. Timber piles

    2. Within the above classifications bearing piles shall be grouped by lengths in increments of 1.00 m and the number of piles in each grouping shall be stated.

    3. Battered piles shall be measured separately, stating the angle of batter.

    4. Splicing and lengthening piles, where required, shall be enumerated, stating the additional length.

    5. Sheet piles shall be measured in square metres on the net (undeveloped) areas to be supported. The rates shall include permanent and temporary supports and cutting.

02450 - FOUNDATION AND LOAD-BEARING ELEMENTS (Continued)

2.   02455 - Driven piles (Continued)

    6.   Rates for concrete filled steel piles shall include excavation and filling within the casing.

    7.   Test piling shall be measured separately. Setting up over each pile, and testing, shall be enumerated.

    8.   Piling to be extracted shall be measured in accordance with the above principles. Disposal of the extracted material shall be described.

3.   02465 - Bored piles

    1.   Piling shall be classified as follows:

        1.   Auger cast group piles
        2.   Bored and belled concrete piles
        3.   Bored and socketed piles
        4.   Bored friction concrete piles
        5.   Drilled caissons
        6.   Uncased cast-in-place concrete piles

    2.   The method of measurement described above for 02455 - Driven piles shall apply, as applicable, to bored piles.

    3.   The expansion or other treatment of the base of the pile, where required, is to be included in the description of the pile.

4.   02475 - Caissons

    1.   Caissons shall be measured in accordance with the rules for the relevant item, i.e. excavation, concrete, etc., set out in this Method of Measurement.

02500 - UTILITY SERVICES

1. Utility services shall be measured in the following categories:

    02510 - Water distribution
    02520 - Wells
    02530 - Sanitary sewage
    02540 - Septic tank systems
    02550 - Piped energy distribution
    02580 - Electrical and communication structures

2. Utility services shall be measured in this Division up to 1.00 m from the outside face of the structure.

3. Pipes, culverts and ducts shall be measured in metres; no deduction shall be made in pipe lengths for fittings not exceeding 225 mm in diameter. Fittings, valves, hydrants, valve boxes, pumps, cisterns, thrust and anchor blocks, drainage bends, junctions, connections and the like, catch-basins, sump pits, manholes, pull boxes etc., shall be enumerated.

4. Drilling or jetting wells shall be measured in metres. Disinfecting water mains shall be stated as an item.

5. Connection charges shall be stated as an item.

6. Septic and similar interceptor tanks, concrete slabs etc. shall be measured in accordance with the rules for the relevant items in this Method of Measurement.

02600 - DRAINAGE AND CONTAINMENT

1. Drainage and containment shall be measured in the following categories:

    02610 - Pipe culverts
    02620 - Subdrainage
    02630 - Storm drainage
    02640 - Culverts and manufactured construction
    02660 - Ponds and reservoirs

2. Drainage shall be measured in this Division up to 1.00 m from the outside face of the structure.

02600 - DRAINAGE AND CONTAINMENT (Continued)

3. Pipe culverts and drainage pipes shall be measured in metres; no deduction shall be made in pipe lengths for bends, junctions etc. not exceeding 225 mm in diameter. Bends, junctions, connections, catch-basins, sump pits, manholes shall be enumerated.

4. Connection charges shall be stated as an item.

5. Interceptor tanks, concrete slabs, manufactured culverts, ponds, reservoirs, etc. shall be measured in accordance with the rules for the relevant items in this Method of Measurement.

02700 - BASES, BALLASTS, PAVEMENTS AND APPURTENANCES

1. Bases, ballasts, pavements and appurtenances shall be measured in the following categories:

   02710 - Bound base courses
   02720 - Unbound base courses and ballasts
   02730 - Aggregate surfacing
   02740 - Flexible paving
   02750 - Rigid pavement
   02760 - Paving specialties
   02770 - Curbs and gutters
   02775 - Sidewalks
   02780 - Unit pavers
   02785 - Flexible pavement coating and micro-sealing
   02790 - Athletic and recreational surfaces
   02795 - Porous pavement

2. Bound and unbound base courses and ballasts shall be measured in cubic metres and shall include all rolling and compacting.

3. Surfacing, paving and sidewalks shall be measured in square metres; curbs and gutters shall be measured in metres. Cutting back the edge of existing pavement, where specifically required, shall be measured in metres. Pavement marking shall be measured in metres, or shall be enumerated, as appropriate.

4. Paving and surfacing to slopes exceeding 30° from the horizontal shall be so described.

02800 - SITE IMPROVEMENTS AND AMENITIES

1. Site improvements and amenities shall be measured in the following categories:

   02810 - Irrigation system
   02815 - Fountains
   02820 - Fences and gates
   02830 - Retaining walls
   02840 - Walk, road and parking appurtenances
   02870 - Site furnishings
   02875 - Site and street shelters
   02880 - Play field equipment and structures
   02890 - Traffic signs and signals

2. Pipes in irrigation systems shall be measured in metres. Bends, junctions, connections etc. shall be deemed to be included in the measurement of the pipe. Sprinklers, valves, controls etc. shall be enumerated.

3. Fences, guard rails, barriers etc. shall be measured in metres. Gates shall be enumerated. Post holes and concrete, or other filling, shall be enumerated.

4. Other manufactured items within these categories shall be enumerated, unless another form of measurement is appropriate for a specific item. Contractor built items shall be measured in accordance with the rules for the relevant material in this Method of Measurement.

02900 - PLANTING

1. Planting shall be measured in the following categories:

   02905 - Transplanting
   02910 - Plant preparation
   02920 - Lawns and grasses
   02930 - Exterior plants
   02935 - Plant maintenance
   02945 - Planting accessories

2. Topsoil, seeding, sodding, other surface treatments and maintenance shall be measured in square metres. Work carried out to slopes exceeding 30° from the horizontal shall be so described.

3. Ground covers, plants, shrubs and trees shall be enumerated.

4. Landscape edging shall be measured in metres, tree grates shall be enumerated.

GENERALLY

1. The section "General Rules" is to be read in conjunction with this Division

2. The major items in this Division shall be measured in the following units unless otherwise stated:

    1. formwork in square metres
    2. reinforcing steel in kilograms and welded wire fabric in square metres
    3. concrete in cubic metres.

03100 - CONCRETE FORMS AND ACCESSORIES

1. Concrete forms and accessories shall be measured in the following categories:

    03110 - Structural cast-in-place concrete forms
    03120 - Architectural cast-in-place concrete forms
    03130 - Permanent forms
    03150 - Concrete accessories

2. Formwork shall be measured to the actual surface in contact with the concrete. The function of the concrete shall be described, e.g. footing, column, wall.

3. No deductions shall be made for openings not exceeding 10.00 m^2, nor for the intersection of beams, slab bands, walls etc.

4. All temporary supports, bracing, strutting, re-shoring, scaffolding, guard rails, walkways and general falsework shall form part of the items of work to which they relate, and shall not be measured separately.

5. All form ties of whatever type, cutting back ties and grouting holes, form oil, fixings, plywood, studs, wailers, stripping, cleaning, oiling, lifting, transporting and any other labour or material necessary for the construction of the concrete formwork shall form part of the item to which they relate, and shall not be measured separately.

6. Notching and boring formwork shall not be measured.

7. Formwork to concrete surfaces not exceeding 200 mm wide or deep shall be measured in metres.

8. Formwork to circular columns shall be measured in metres.

03100 - CONCRETE FORMS AND ACCESSORIES (Continued)

9. Designed indents, rebates, fillets, coves, arrises, mouldings, block-outs, etc., which are attached to the face of the formwork, shall be measured in metres. Such items not exceeding 300 mm in length shall be enumerated.

10. Small items attached to formwork, such as inserts, anchors, plates, pipe cones, etc., shall be enumerated.

11. Items which are at the discretion of the contractor, such as pour strips, shall not be measured.

12. Formwork which is single sided shall be so described.

13. Formwork to confined spaces shall be kept separate.

14. Scribing formwork to rock face or profile shall be measured in metres.

15. Formwork to walls and columns exceeding 3.50 m in height shall be measured separately in 1.50 m increments.

16. Formwork to underside of suspended slabs, to soffits of slab bands, column heads, drop panels and to sides and soffits of beams, shall each be grouped according to height. Where over 3.50 m high, the height shall be stated in increments of 1.50 m.

17. Anchors and inserts shall be enumerated; expansion and contraction joints, waterstops and the like shall be measured in metres.

03200 - CONCRETE REINFORCEMENT

1. Concrete reinforcement shall be measured in the following categories:

    03210 - Reinforcing steel
    03220 - Welded wire fabric
    03230 - Stressing tendons
    03250 - Post tensioning

2. Reinforcing steel shall be classified by size, each size being given separately. The full length including laps, bends and hooks shall be measured. Tying wire, distance blocks and ordinary spacers shall be deemed to be included, and the weight of such items shall not be added to the weight of the reinforcing steel.

03200 - CONCRETE REINFORCEMENT (Continued)

3. Within each size classification main reinforcing steel shall be further classified as straight, or with up to four bends per bar. Stirrups and links shall be so described and shall be deemed to include up to five bends per bar. Reinforcing steel which falls outside the number of bends in these categories shall be separately described.

4. Reinforcing steel in lengths exceeding 13.00 m shall be kept separate.

5. Welded wire fabric shall be measured as the area covered. No deduction shall be made for voids not exceeding 1.00 m^2. Tying wire and distance blocks shall be deemed to be included.

6. Stressing tendons for post-tensioned concrete shall be measured with category 03380.

03300 - CAST-IN-PLACE CONCRETE

1. Cast-in-place concrete shall be measured in the following categories:

    03310 - Structural concrete
    03330 - Architectural concrete
    03340 - Low density concrete
    03350 - Concrete finishing
    03360 - Concrete finishes
    03370 - Specially placed concrete
    03380 - Post-tensioned concrete
    03390 - Concrete curing

2. No deduction shall be made for concrete displaced by other materials cast into the concrete, nor for openings not exceeding 0.05 m^3 in volume.

3. Concrete that, by reason of its location or nature, must be pumped or continuously poured, or specifically compacted or vibrated, shall be so described.

4. Integral admixtures to concrete shall be measured in cubic metres as extra over the cost of concrete to be so treated.

5. Concrete finishing, concrete finishes and concrete curing shall be measured in square metres.

03300 - CAST-IN-PLACE CONCRETE (Continued)

6. All work associated with post-tensioned concrete shall be measured under a separate heading, with the constituent parts measured in accordance with the foregoing principles. Cables which are to be tensioned, and tube ducts shall be measured in metres. Separate items shall be given for initial tensioning, for pressure grouting, and for additional tensioning if required. Grouting prestressing tendons shall be enumerated.

03400 - PRECAST CONCRETE

1. Precast concrete shall be measured in the following categories:

   03410 - Plant-precast structural concrete
   03420 - Plant-precast structural post-tensioned concrete
   03430 - Site-precast structural concrete
   03450 - Plant-precast architectural concrete
   03460 - Site-precast architectural concrete
   03470 - Tilt-up precast concrete
   03480 - Precast concrete specialties

2. Formwork and reinforcement shall not be measured separately but shall be described with the item.

3. Slabs, walls, covers etc. shall be measured in square metres. Beams, sills, copings, etc. shall be measured in metres. Individual items shall be enumerated.

4. Structural precast post-tensioned concrete shall be measured in the same manner as post-tensioned cast-in-place concrete, as described in 03300 – Cast-in-Place Concrete, item 6 above.

03500 - CEMENTITIOUS DECKS AND UNDERLAYMENT

1. Cementitious decks and underlayment shall be measured in the following categories:

   03510 - Cementitious roof deck
   03520 - Lightweight concrete roof insulation
   03530 - Concrete topping
   03540 - Cementitious underlayment

2. All work in this category shall be measured in square metres.

03600 - GROUTS

1. Grouting shall be measured in metres, or may be enumerated, as appropriate.

03900 - CONCRETE RESTORATION AND CLEANING

1. Concrete restoration and cleaning shall be measured in the following categories:

    03910 - Concrete cleaning
    03920 - Concrete resurfacing
    03930 - Concrete rehabilitation

2. Work in this category shall normally be measured in square metres.

GENERALLY

1. The section "General Rules" is to be read in conjunction with this Division.

2. The major items of masonry work shall be measured in square metres. No deductions shall be made for openings not exceeding 1.00 m^2.

3. The measurement of masonry shall be deemed to include normal cleaning, building in or cutting chases for pipes, ducts and conduits, for cutting around, against and to the underside of concrete or steel members, and building in anchor bolts, sleeves, brackets and similar items. Special sized units to allow bonding with other materials shall also be deemed included.

4. Masonry shall be measured under the following headings:

   1. Facings
   2. Backings to facings
   3. Walls and partitions
   4. Furring to walls
   5. Fire protection to structural steelwork
   6. Chimney stacks
   7. Damp courses

5. Sections (04060) - Mortar materials and (04070) – Grout, used in the installation of masonry shall be included in the measurement of the masonry item.

04080 - MASONRY ANCHORAGE AND REINFORCEMENT

1. Joint reinforcement shall be measured in metres.

2. Ties, shoe tile units, anchors and the like shall be enumerated.

3. Reinforcing steel shall be measured in kilograms or metres.

4. Setting only steel lintels shall be measured in kilograms and the number shall be stated.

04090 - MASONRY ACCESSORIES

1. Control and expansion joints shall be measured in metres.

2. Embedded flashings integral with masonry shall be measured in metres.

04200 - MASONRY UNITS

1. Unit masonry shall be measured in the following categories:

    04210 - Clay masonry units
    04220 - Concrete masonry units
    04230 - Reinforced unit masonry
    04270 - Glass masonry units

2. Reinforced block and tile lintels shall be measured in metres.

3. Masonry units in special shapes shall be enumerated.

4. The formation of decorative patterns and features shall be measured in square metres as "extra labour and material", describing the decorative pattern or feature.

5. Special units of differing thickness from the main unit, where required at sills, heads and the like, shall be measured in metres.

6. Chimney caps shall be enumerated.

7. Silicone treatment to the surface of masonry shall be measured in square metres.

04400 - STONE

1. Stone shall be measured in the following categories:

    04410 - Natural and cut stone
    04420 - Collected stone
    04430 - Quarried stone

2. Copings, sills, jambs, mullions and the like shall be measured in metres.

3. Keystones, isolated lettered stones, and similar individual items shall be enumerated.

04500 - REFRACTORIES

1. Refractories shall be measured in the following categories:

   04550 - Flue liners
   04560 - Combustion chambers
   04580 - Refractory brick

2. Flue liners shall be measured in metres. Combustion chambers shall be measured in square metres, with the floor, walls and roof kept separate. Alternatively, combustion chambers may be enumerated. Refractory brick shall be measured in square metres.

04600 - CORROSION RESISTANT MASONRY

1. Corrosion resistant masonry shall be measured in the following categories:

   04610 - Chemical resistant brick
   04620 - Vitrified clay liner plates

2. Chemical resistant brick and vitrified clay liner plates shall be measured in accordance with the Method of Measurement for Masonry Units.

04700 - SIMULATED MASONRY

1. Mineral, epoxy, fibreglass and other types of simulated masonry shall be measured in accordance with the Method of Measurement for Masonry Units.

04900 - MASONRY RESTORATION AND CLEANING

1. Masonry restoration, alterations and cleaning shall be measured in the following categories:

   04910 - Unit masonry restoration
   04920 - Stone restoration
   04930 - Unit masonry cleaning
   04940 - Stone cleaning

2. The type of masonry shall be described. Interior and exterior work shall be measured separately.

3. Cutting openings shall be enumerated.

4. Making good jambs to new openings shall be measured in metres.

04900 - MASONRY RESTORATION AND CLEANING (Continued)

5. Cutting, toothing and bonding new work to existing shall be measured in metres.

6. Blocking up existing openings shall be enumerated.

7. Masonry work in raising old walls shall be kept separate, and the height above ground stated. Preparation of existing walls for raising shall be measured in metres.

8. Shoring and needling, or propping for insertion of new lintels shall be enumerated, stating the size of the opening, and thickness of the wall.

GENERALLY

1.   The section "General Rules" is to be read in conjunction with this Division.

2.   Unless otherwise stated, structural steel shall be measured by mass in tonnes or kilograms.   The weight of structural sections shall be calculated from the theoretical mass of the section as detailed by the Canadian Institute of Steel Construction.

05100 - STRUCTURAL METAL FRAMING

1.   Structural metal framing shall be measured in the following categories:

     05120 - Structural steel
     05140 - Structural aluminum
     05150 - Wire rope assemblies
     05160 - Metal framing systems

2.   Within these categories, as appropriate, each differing structural section shall be given separately and described in accordance with its function, e.g. column, beam, member of roof truss, etc. Members of a built-up section shall be grouped under a suitable heading.

3.   Metal fastenings for joining metals together shall be given by mass, and grouped as rivets, welds, or bolts, nuts and washers.

4.   The overall length, depth, span and load capacity of open web joists shall be given.

05200 - METAL JOISTS

1.   Non-framed metal joists shall be measured in the following categories:

     05210 - Steel joists
     05250 - Aluminum joists
     05260 - Composite joist assemblies

2.   Related bridging, anchors and accessories shall be included with these categories.

05300 - METAL DECK

1. Metal deck shall be measured in the following categories:

    05310 - Steel deck
    05320 - Raceway deck systems
    05330 - Aluminum deck
    05340 - Acoustical metal deck

2. Metal decking shall be measured in square metres. Raking and circular cutting shall each be measured in metres.

3. Gutters, eavestroughs, end fillers and other special shapes shall be measured in metres. Ends, mitres, junctions etc., shall be enumerated.

4. Holes, notches, pipe flashings, etc. shall be enumerated.

05400 - COLD-FORMED METAL FRAMING

1. Cold-formed metal framing shall be measured in the following categories:

    05410 - Load-bearing metal studs
    05420 - Cold-formed metal joists
    05450 - Metal supports

2. Load-bearing metal stud walls and partitions shall be measured in square metres.

3. Cold-formed metal joists shall be measured in metres.

4. Metal supports shall be enumerated.

05500 - METAL FABRICATIONS

1. Metal fabrications shall be measured in the following categories:

    05510 - Metal stairs and ladders
    05520 - Handrails and railings
    05530 - Gratings
    05540 - Floor plates
    05550 - Stair treads and nosings
    05560 - Castings

05500 - METAL FABRICATIONS (Continued)

2.   The components of metal stairs shall be grouped under a brief description of the stairs; the description shall include the method of fabrication. The individual components shall be measured in metres, or enumerated, as appropriate.

3.   Ladders shall be enumerated.

4.   Handrails and railings shall be measured in metres. Handrail brackets shall be enumerated.

5.   Gratings, floor plates, stair treads and nosings shall be measured in metres.

6.   Castings shall be measured in metres, or enumerated, as appropriate.

05700 - ORNAMENTAL METAL

1.   Ornamental metal shall be measured in the following categories:

     05710 - Ornamental stairs
     05715 - Prefabricated spiral stairs
     05720 - Ornamental handrails and railings
     05725 - Ornamental metal castings
     05730 - Ornamental sheet metal

2.   Items in the above categories shall be measured in accordance with the principles set out in Section 05500 - Metal fabrications.

05800 - EXPANSION CONTROL

1.   Expansion control shall be measured in the following categories:

     05810 - Expansion joint cover assemblies
     05820 - Slide bearings
     05830 - Bridge expansion joint assemblies

2.   Items in the above categories shall be measured in metres, or enumerated, as appropriate.

GENERALLY

1. The section "General Rules" is to be read in conjunction with this Division.

2. Lumber and finishing trim shall be measured in metres unless otherwise stated. Building paper and felt, wood, plywood and board sheathing, soffits and panelling shall be measured in square metres. Small blockings, backboards and the like shall be enumerated. Rough hardware fixings, other than nails and screws, shall be enumerated; drilling through wood and other materials in this Division shall be deemed included in the fixing item.

3. The dimensions of lumber shall be given as finished metric sizes,

4. Lumber specified to be in lengths exceeding 6.00 m shall be kept separate and given in 1.00 m stages.

5. Fasteners shall be enumerated within each category.

6. The treatment of wood products to increase their durability, retard burning and prevent attack by insects shall be described with the item, or group of items, to which the treatment applies.

06100 - ROUGH CARPENTRY

1. Rough carpentry shall be measured in the following categories:

    06110 - Wood framing
    06120 - Structural panels
    06130 - Heavy timber construction
    06140 - Treated wood foundations
    06150 - Wood decking
    06160 - Sheathing
    06170 - Prefabricated structural wood
    06180 - Glued-laminated construction

06100 - ROUGH CARPENTRY (Continued)

2. Additional information shall be given in the description of particular items within the above categories as follows:

  1. 06110 - Wood framing

    1. Stud walls exceeding 3.00 m in height shall be so described, and shall be kept separate in 1.00 m increments

    2. Bridging shall be measured over the joists and the depth and centres of the joists shall be stated.

  2. 06130 - Heavy timber construction

    1. The individual components of timber trusses shall be kept separate.

  3. 06150 - Wood decking

    1. Work in this category is normally material which remains exposed.

  4. 06160 - Sheathing

    1. Work to sloping or pitched surfaces exceeding 10° shall be kept separate, stating the pitch

    2. Diagonal work shall be kept separate

    3. Gypsum sheathing over or under wood framing, when used as an unfinished fire stop, is included in this category.

  5. 06170 - Prefabricated structural wood

    1. Wood chord metal joists shall be measured in metres.

    2. Prefabricated wood trusses shall be enumerated.

06200 - FINISH CARPENTRY

1.   Finish carpentry shall be measured in the following categories:

> 06220 - Millwork
> 06250 - Prefinished paneling
> 06260 - Board paneling
> 06270 - Closet and utility wood shelving

2.   The above categories include the fabrication and installation of site built and site finished cabinets, moulding and trim and the installation of cabinet hardware.

3.   Shelving exceeding 300 mm wide, and slatted shelving, shall be measured in square metres.

4.   Wood, composition, plywood and plastic siding may be measured in the above categories instead of in Division 7.

06400 - ARCHITECTURAL WOODWORK

1.   Architectural woodwork shall be measured in the following categories:

> 06410 - Custom cabinets
> 06415 - Countertops
> 06420 - Paneling
> 06430 - Wood stairs and railings
> 06450 - Standing and running trim
> 06460 - Wood frames
> 06470 - Screens, blinds and shutters

2.   The above categories include the shop fabrication and prefinishing of woodwork requiring expert craftsmanship and joinery, and the installation of fasteners and hardware.

3.   Custom casework, comprising plastic laminate faced, shop finished or unfinished wood cabinets shall be enumerated.

4.   Stairwork comprising treads, risers, nosings, balusters and newel posts shall be enumerated.

06500 - STRUCTURAL PLASTICS

1. Structural plastic framing elements, and other plastic fabrications, including erection and anchorage, shall be measured in this category.

2. The method of measurement shall be the same as for the comparable items described previously in this Division.

06600 - PLASTIC FABRICATIONS

1. Construction units and assemblies using plastic material shall be measured in this category.

2. The method of measurement shall be the same as for the comparable items described previously in this Division.

06900 - WOOD AND PLASTIC RESTORATION AND CLEANING

1. Wood and plastic restoration and cleaning shall be measured in the following categories:

    06910 - Wood restoration and cleaning
    06920 - Plastic restoration and cleaning

2. Work in this category may be measured in metres, square metres, or enumerated as appropriate.

GENERALLY

1. The section "General Rules" is to be read in conjunction with this Division.

2. Unless otherwise stated, all items in this Division shall be measured in square metres.

3. Vertical, horizontal, sloped, curved surfaces and areas inside tanks shall be measured separately.

4. In respect to roofing, the nature of the surface to receive the roofing, and the height above grade at which the work will be executed, shall be given.

5. Special testing procedures, where required, shall be given, stating the number of tests to be undertaken, the method of test execution and subsequent repair.

07100 - DAMPPROOFING AND WATERPROOFING

1. Dampproofing refers to materials which are not subject to hydrostatic pressure, while waterproofing refers to materials which are subject to continuous or intermittent hydrostatic pressure. Dampproofing and waterproofing shall be measured in the following categories:

    07110 - Dampproofing
    07120 - Built-up bituminous waterproofing
    07130 - Sheet waterproofing
    07140 - Fluid-applied waterproofing
    07150 - Sheet metal waterproofing
    07170 - Bentonite waterproofing
    07180 - Traffic coatings
    07190 - Water repellents

2. Protection covering shall be measured separately.

3. Deductions shall be made for openings exceeding 4.00 m^2.

4. Work to reglets, chases and similar items shall be measured in metres.

5. Work around, or openings for, pipes, sleeves, drains, bolts or other similar items shall be enumerated.

6. The material to which water repellent is to be applied shall be stated.

07200 - THERMAL PROTECTION

1. Thermal protection shall be measured under the following categories:

    07210 - Building insulation
    07220 - Roof and deck insulation
    07240 - Exterior insulation and finish systems (EIFS)
    07260 - Vapour retarders
    07270 - Air barriers

2. Deductions shall be made for openings exceeding 4.00 m^2.

3. The location to which the thermal insulation is to be applied shall be stated.

4. Insulation placed inside formwork shall be so stated.

5. Insulation placed by blowing shall be so stated.

6. Sprayed insulation exceeding 4.00 m high shall be measured separately.

7. Composite exterior insulation and finish systems shall be measured as one item, and described as site or shop applied.

07300 - SHINGLES, ROOF TILES AND ROOF COVERINGS

1. Shingles, roof tiles and roof coverings shall be measured in the following categories:

    07310 - Shingles
    07320 - Roof tiles
    07330 - Roof coverings

2. Deduction shall be made for openings exceeding 1.00 m^2.

3. The component parts of shingle roofing, i.e. preparatory work, sheathing paper, underlayment and surfacing shall be given.

4. The component parts of tile roofing i.e. preparatory work, sheathing paper, underlayment, fixing media and surfacing shall be given.

07400 - ROOFING AND SIDING PANELS

1. Manufactured roofing and siding shall be measured in the following categories:

    07410 - Manufactured roof and wall panels
    07420 - Plastic roof and wall panels
    07430 - Composite panels
    07440 - Faced panels
    07450 - Fibre-reinforced cementitious panels
    07460 - Siding
    07470 - Wood roof and wall panels
    07480 - Exterior wall assemblies

2. Wood, plywood, composition and plastic sidings may be measured in Division 6, category 06200.

07500 - MEMBRANE ROOFING

1. Membrane roofing shall be measured in the following categories:

    07510 - Built-up bituminous roofing
    07520 - Cold-applied bituminous roofing
    07530 - Elastomeric membrane roofing
    07540 - Thermoplastic membrane roofing
    07550 - Modified bituminous membrane roofing
    07560 - Fluid-applied roofing
    07570 - Coated foamed roofing
    07580 - Roll roofing
    07590 - Roof maintenance and repairs

2. The component parts of membrane roofing i.e. preparatory work, sheathing paper, primer, vapour barrier, underlayment, insulation, felt, asphalt, membrane, surfacing, gravel, as applicable to the particular material, shall be given.

07600 - FLASHING AND SHEET METAL

1.   Flashing and sheet metal shall be measured in the following categories:

     07610 - Sheet metal roofing
     07620 - Sheet metal flashing and trim
     07630 - Sheet metal roofing specialties
     07650 - Flexible flashing

2.   The component parts of sheet metal roofing, i.e. preparatory work, sheathing paper, primer, underlayment, surfacing shall be given.

3.   Standing seams, welts and drips forming part of the general roof area shall be given in the item of roofing.

4.   Flashing, gutters, valleys, hips, starter and underlayment strips, cants, etc., shall be separately measured in metres.

07700 - ROOF SPECIALITIES AND ACCESSORIES

1.   Roof specialties and accessories shall be measured in the following categories:

     07710 - Manufactured roof specialties
     07720 - Roof accessories
     07730 - Roof pavers

2.   Copings, counterflashing systems, gravel stops, fascias, reglets and the like, shall be separately measured in metres.

3.   Roof hatches, vents, scuppers and the like shall be separately enumerated.

4.   Roof pavers shall be measured in square metres.

07800 - FIRE AND SMOKE PROTECTION

1.   Fire and smoke protection shall be measured in the following categories:

     07810 - Applied fireproofing
     07820 - Board fireproofing
     07840 - Firestopping

2.   Fire and smoke protection shall be measured in metres or in square metres as appropriate.

07900 - JOINT SEALERS

1.   Joint sealers shall be measured in the following categories:

>   07910 - Preformed joint seals
>   07920 - Joint sealants

2.   Joint fillers, gaskets and caulking shall be separately measured in metres. Where special equipment methods are required to be employed, this shall be given.

GENERALLY

1.   The section "General Rules" is to be read in conjunction with this Division.

2.   Unless otherwise stated all items in this Division shall be enumerated.

3.   Temporary supports, bracing and protection of components prior to building in shall be measured as a separate item.

4.   Final cleaning of units shall be measured as a separate item.

5.   Wood surfaces to receive a clear finish shall be so described.

6.   Any testing shall be measured as a separate item.

7.   Hardware items, unless part of a pre-packaged assembly, shall be measured in Section 08700 - Hardware.

8.   Glazing and glazing accessories may be included with the appropriate door, or may be measured in Section 08800 - Glazing.

9.   Wood frames, which are not provided as part of Section 08250 - Door Opening Assemblies, shall be measured in Division 6.

10.   A description of blockings and stiffeners to accommodate finishing hardware shall be included in the description of doors.

11.   Blanking out, reinforcing, drilling and tapping to receive standard and heavy duty mortise hinges, closers, keeps, etc. from templates received from the finishing hardware supplier, together with removable stops, mutes, plaster grounds and anchors shall be included in the description of frames.

08100 - METAL DOORS AND FRAMES

1.   Metal doors and frames shall be measured in the following categories:

       08110 - Steel doors and frames
       08120 - Aluminum doors and frames
       08130 - Stainless steel doors and frames
       08140 - Bronze doors and frames
       08150 - Preassembled metal door and frame units
       08160 - Sliding metal doors and grilles
       08180 - Metal screen and storm doors

2   08100 - METAL DOORS AND FRAMES (Continued)

2. Louvres fabricated integrally with doors and frames shall be described with the appropriate door or frame. Louvres which are field inserted in doors and frames shall be measured for supply under Divisions 10 or 15, and shall be enumerated for fixing only in this Section.

3. Combination frames, incorporating side and transom lights, shall be measured in metres under their constituent parts, i.e. frame, transom, mullion, sill. Connections between each part shall be enumerated, by type.

4. The installation of doors, frames and combination frames shall each be enumerated separately.

08200 - WOOD AND PLASTIC DOORS

1. Wood and plastic doors shall be measured in the following categories:

    08210 - Wood doors
    08220 - Plastic doors
    08250 - Preassembled wood and plastic door and frame units
    08260 - Sliding wood and plastic doors
    08280 - Wood and plastic storm and screen doors

2. Wood louvres and factory installed metal louvres for fire rated doors shall be described with the appropriate door. Metal louvres which are field inserted in non-fire rated doors shall be measured for supply in Divisions 10 or 15, and shall be enumerated for fixing only in this Section.

3. The installation of doors shall be separately enumerated.

08300 - SPECIALTY DOORS

1. Specialty doors and assemblies, including hardware, controls, operators and drive mechanisms shall be measured in the following categories:

   08310 - Access doors and panels
   08320 - Detention doors and frames
   08330 - Coiling doors and grilles
   08340 - Special function doors
   08350 - Folding doors and grilles
   08360 - Overhead doors
   08370 - Vertical lift doors
   08380 - Traffic doors
   08390 - Pressure-resistant doors

2. The installation of special doors shall each be separately enumerated.

08400 - ENTRANCES AND STOREFRONTS

1. Entrances and storefronts are typically one storey systems. Each shall be measured separately, for supply and installation, in the following categories:

   08410 - Metal-framed storefronts
   08450 - All-glass entrances and storefronts
   08460 - Automatic entrance doors
   08470 - Revolving entrance doors
   08480 - Balanced entrance doors
   08490 - Sliding storefronts

2. Within each category, each section shall be preceded by a descriptive preamble which shall include a short description of the components, the overall dimensions of the unit and the material to which it will be fixed.

3. Glass and glazing shall be measured in accordance with Section 08800. Alternatively, where appropriate, glass and glazing may be included with the description of the entrance or storefront.

4. Entrance doors, screens, automatic door operators, metal anchors and the like shall be enumerated. Door thresholds shall be measured in metres and the number stated. Handrails shall be measured in metres. Special facings shall be measured in square metres and shall include the supporting framework. Structural steel reinforcing members shall be measured in kilograms.

08400 - ENTRANCES AND STOREFRONTS (Continued)

5. Storefronts shall be measured in accordance with the methods of measurement in the preceding paragraph as far as they apply. Spandrel and infill panels shall be enumerated. Insulation applied in the field shall be measured in square metres. Window cleaning anchors, including reinforcement, shall be enumerated. Hoisting, if the responsibility of this contractor, shall be given as an item.

08500 - WINDOWS

1. Windows shall be measured in the following categories:

   08510 - Steel windows
   08520 - Aluminum windows
   08530 - Stainless steel windows
   08540 - Bronze windows
   08550 - Wood windows
   08560 - Plastic windows
   08570 - Composite windows
   08580 - Special function windows

2. Fixed and operable windows used singly, or in multiples, shall be enumerated separately. The method of operation of operable windows, (sliding, hung, etc.), shall be given in the description.

3. Window units with louvre blinds set integrally between glass panels shall be so described.

4. Jalousies shall be enumerated.

5. Components such as main frame, mullion, transom, sill shall be measured separately, in metres. Connections between components shall be enumerated, by type.

6. Where windows are factory glazed, the glazing beads, glass and glazing, and solar plastic film if required, shall be included with the window. Otherwise, glazing beads shall be described with the window, and glass and glazing shall be measured in Section 08800.

7. The installation of windows shall be enumerated, stating overall size, and whether installed from the outside or inside.

08600 - SKYLIGHTS

1.   Skylights shall be measured in the following categories:

> 08610 - Roof windows
> 08620 - Unit skylights
> 08630 - Metal-framed skylights

08700 - HARDWARE

1.   Hardware shall be measured in the following categories:

> 08710 - Door hardware
> 08720 - Weatherstripping and seals
> 08740 - Electro-mechanical hardware
> 08750 - Window hardware
> 08770 - Door and window accessories
> 08790 - Special function hardware

2.   Hardware and gasketing for doors and windows not specifically supplied as part of the manufactured item shall be measured in this Section. (Note: Hardware required for items supplied in Divisions 6, 10 and 12 shall be included with those Divisions.)

3.   The installation of hardware shall normally be measured separately from its supply.

4.   Matching screws shall be deemed to be included in the supply of hardware.

5.   Preparing wood, metal, etc., to receive hardware (e.g. sinking, boring, grooving, mortising,) shall be deemed to be included with the appropriate installation item.

6.   Butts and hinges shall be measured in pairs.

7.   Weatherstripping shall be measured in metres.

8.   Keying of locks shall be given as a separate item stating number of keys per item, master keying and any requirement to match an existing system.

08800 - GLAZING

1. Glass and glazing shall be measured in the following categories:

    08810 - Glass
    08830 - Mirrors
    08840 - Plastic glazing
    08850 - Glazing accessories

2. All types of glass and glazing used for doors, windows, sidelights, transoms, entrances, storefronts, curtain walls, framed skylights and balustrades not specifically supplied as part of the manufactured item shall be measured in this Section.

3. Glass and plastic glazing shall be measured in square metres. Each light shall be measured to the next increment of 20 mm in each direction for either single glass or sealed units.

4. Lights of glass of irregular shape shall be measured to the nearest rectangular area, in accordance with the previous paragraph, and described as "in irregular areas." Circular cutting shall be measured in metres.

5. Lights of glass which are bent shall be enumerated, and the radius of the bend stated.

6. Interior and exterior glass and glazing shall be given separately. If scaffolding or special hoisting is required, this shall be stated.

7. Setting blocks, shims, splines, clips and other accessories shall be deemed to be included in the description of glass and glazing.

8. Glazing compound, tape, and the removal and refixing of glazing beads shall be measured in metres.

9. Edge work shall be measured in metres.

10. Holes drilled or cut in glass shall be enumerated, giving details of the hole and the glass.

11. Grinding, sandblasting, acid etching, embossing, etc., shall be enumerated.

12. The length of guarantee for sealed units shall be stated.

08800 – GLAZING (Continued)

13.   Stained glass work and solar plastic film shall be measured in Division 12.

14.   Glazing integral with casework, food service equipment, telephone enclosures and detention equipment is measured with the item in the appropriate Division.

08900 - GLAZED CURTAIN WALL

1.   Glazed curtain walls are typically designed for multistorey construction but may be applied to single storey structures. They shall be measured for supply and installation in the following categories:

        08910 - Metal framed curtain walls
        08950 - Translucent wall and roof assemblies
        08960 - Sloped glazing assemblies
        08970 - Structural glass curtain walls

2.   Within each category, each section shall be preceded by a descriptive preamble which shall include a short description of the components, the overall dimensions of the unit and the material to which it will be fixed.

3.   Glass and glazing shall be measured in accordance with Section 08800. Alternatively, where appropriate, glass and glazing may be included with the description of the curtain wall.

4.   The principles of measurement previously described in Section 08100 - Metal doors and frames, and 08500 - Windows shall apply equally to this Section.

5.   Spandrel and infill panels shall be enumerated.

6.   Insulation applied in the field shall be measured in square metres. Hoisting, if the responsibility of this contractor, shall be given as an item.

GENERALLY

1.   The section "General Rules" is to be read in conjunction with this Division.

2.   Finishes shall be measured in square metres.

3.   Work exceeding 4.00 m high shall be so described, and the height above the floor level given in 2.00 m stages.

4.   Where not otherwise apparent, work in this Division shall be stated to be either to floors, walls or ceilings.

5.   Where work to landings is required to be stated, it refers to landings not exceeding 4.00 m^2. Landings exceeding 4.00 m^2 shall be considered to be floors.

6.   Exterior work shall be so stated.

09100 - METAL SUPPORT ASSEMBLIES

1.   Metal support assemblies shall be measured in the following categories:

     09110 - Non-load-bearing wall framing
     09120 - Ceiling suspension
     09130 - Acoustical suspension

2.   Deductions shall be made for openings exceeding 2.00 m^2.

09200 - PLASTER AND GYPSUM BOARD

1.   Plaster and gypsum board shall be measured in the following categories:

     09205 - Furring and lathing
     09210 - Gypsum plaster
     09220 - Portland cement plaster
     09230 - Plaster fabrications
     09250 - Gypsum board
     09260 - Gypsum board assemblies

2.   Deductions shall be made for openings exceeding 2.00 m^2.

3.   Plaster and gypsum board to columns, isolated columns, beams, bulkheads, ducts and the like shall be so stated. Where the girth of such work does not exceed 2.00 m, it shall be stated as not exceeding 1.00 m girth, or exceeding 1.00 m but not exceeding 2.00 m girth.

09200 - PLASTER AND GYPSUM BOARD (Continued)

4. Gypsum board not exceeding 300 mm wide, unless caused by voids, shall be so stated.

5. Framings within plaster and gypsum board for recessed openings shall be enumerated.

6. Corner beads, casing beads, joint and strip reinforcement shall be measured in metres.

7. Angle beads, stops, casings, expansion joints, base screeds, wall mouldings and metal extrusions shall be measured in metres.

8. Plaster work to columns, isolated columns and beams shall be so stated.

9. No deductions shall be made for bases, mouldings, grounds, etc.

10. Cornices, mouldings, bases, friezes, etc. shall be measured their extreme length, in metres.

11. Column bases, caps and other enrichments shall be enumerated.

12. Patching in repair work, where partitions, bases, rails, etc. have been removed, shall be measured in metres.

13. Holes, notches, etc. in gypsum board shall be deemed included.

09300 - TILE

1. Tile shall be measured in the following categories:

   09310 - Ceramic tile
   09330 - Quarry tile
   09340 - Paver tile
   09350 - Glass mosaics
   09360 - Plastic tile
   09370 - Metal tile
   09380 - Cut natural stone tile

2. Deductions shall be made for openings exceeding 0.50 m^2.

3. Tiles to floor and walls of swimming and therapeutic pools shall be so described.

09300 – TILE (Continued)

4. Tiles with rounded edges, internal and external angle tiles, coved base tiles, etc. shall be measured in metres.

5. Tiles rounded on two edges shall be enumerated.

6. Built up bases, jambs, treads, risers, scum gutters, etc., shall be measured in metres; special shaped tiles shall be included in the description.

7. Tiles forming letters and numerals shall be enumerated.

8. Tiling to pump bases, and other similar small items, shall be enumerated.

9. Ceramic tile towel bar holders, toilet paper roll holders, soap dishes and other ceramic tile toilet accessories shall be enumerated, and included in this Division.

09400 - TERRAZZO

1. Terrazzo shall be measured in the following categories:

   09410 - Portland cement terrazzo
   09420 - Precast terrazzo
   09430 - Conductive terrazzo
   09440 - Plastic matrix terrazzo

2. Deductions shall be made for openings exceeding $1.00 \ m^2$.

3. Patterned work shall be so stated.

4. Accessories, such as division strips and finish sealers, shall be given in the description. The sizes of panels shall be stated.

5. Curbs and base shall be measured in metres. Base and border shall be measured as one item, in metres.

6. Work to stairs and landings shall be kept separate. Treads and risers shall be measured as one item, in metres, and the number of treads stated. Non-slip nosings, strings and aprons shall each be separately measured in metres.

7. Rebates to receive frames, gratings, and the like shall be measured in metres. Rebates and sinkings for mat frames shall be enumerated.

09400 - TERRAZZO (Continued)

8. Features formed in precast work shall be measured in metres, or enumerated, as appropriate. Holes, notches and the like in precast work shall be enumerated.

9. Small items, in both cast-in-place and precast items, shall be enumerated.

09500 - CEILINGS

1. Ceiling shall be measured in the following categories:

    09510 - Acoustical ceilings
    09545 - Specialty ceilings
    09550 - Mirror panel ceilings
    09560 - Textured ceilings
    09570 - Linear wood ceilings
    09580 - Suspended decorative grids

2. Deductions shall be made for openings exceeding $0.50 \ m^2$.

3. Surfaces not exceeding 300 mm wide, unless caused by voids, shall be measured in metres. Special borders shall be measured in metres.

4. Ceilings to sides and soffits of beams shall be so described. Special corner joints shall be given in metres.

09600 - FLOORING

1. Flooring shall be measured in the following categories:

    09610 - Floor treatment
    09620 - Specialty flooring
    09630 - Masonry flooring
    09650 - Resilient flooring
    09660 - Static control flooring
    09670 - Fluid-applied flooring
    09680 - Carpet

2. Deductions shall be made for openings exceeding $0.50 \ m^2$ in categories 09610, 09620 and 09630, and exceeding $1.00 \ m^2$ in all other categories.

3. Work not exceeding 300 mm wide, unless caused by voids, shall be measured in metres.

09600 - FLOORING (Continued)

4. Base, treads, nosings, risers, feature strips and the like shall be so described and measured in metres.

5. Flooring to decorative patterns, borders, games courts, etc., shall be so described.

6. Carpet to landings shall be so described.

7. Carpet fixing at perimeters shall be measured in metres. Cutting and fitting carpet around obstructions shall be enumerated.

8. Cover and threshold strips shall be measured in metres.

09700 - WALL FINISHES

1. Wall finishes shall be measured in the following categories:

    09710 - Acoustical wall finishes
    09720 - Wall covering
    09730 - Wall carpet
    09740 - Flexible wood sheets
    09750 - Stone facing
    09770 - Special wall surfaces

2. Deductions shall be made for openings exceeding 1.00 m^2.

3. Wall finishes not exceeding 300 mm wide, unless caused by voids, shall be measured in metres.

4. Border strips shall be measured in metres.

09800 - ACOUSTICAL TREATMENT

1. Acoustical treatment shall be measured in the following categories:

    09810 - Acoustical space units
    09820 - Acoustical insulation and sealants
    09830 - Acoustical barriers
    09840 - Acoustical wall treatment

2. Deductions shall be made for openings exceeding 1.00 m^2.

09800 - ACOUSTICAL TREATMENT (Continued)

3.　Surfaces not exceeding 300 mm wide, unless caused by voids, shall be measured in metres. Borders shall be measured in metres.

4.　Acoustical tile to sides and soffits of beams shall be measured in metres; the type of corner joint shall be stated.

5.　Holes, notches and the like shall be deemed included.

09900 - PAINTS AND COATINGS

1.　Paints and coatings shall be measured in the following categories:

>   09910 - Exterior and interior painting
>   09930 - Stains and transparent finishes
>   09940 - Decorative finishes
>   09960 - High-performance coatings
>   09970 - Coatings for steel
>   09980 - Coatings for concrete and masonry

2.　Deductions shall be made for openings exceeding 1.00 m^2.

3.　Work in confined areas shall be so described.

4.　Special decorative work, such as striped colours and dragged or patterned work, shall be so described.

5.　The contact area of the surface to be painted shall be measured. Allowances shall be made for corrugations, tongued and grooved surfaces, etc.

6.　Painting to surfaces not exceeding 300 mm wide, unless caused by voids, shall be measured in metres.

7.　Cut lines between changes of colour shall be measured in metres.

8.　Windows and doors shall be measured overall, both sides; no deduction shall be made for the area of glass.

09900 - PAINTS AND COATINGS (Continued)

9. Balustrades, fencing and similar items shall be measured overall, both sides, between top and bottom rails. The extra area of posts above and below the rails shall be deemed included.

10. Handrails and similar items shall be measured in metres; brackets shall be deemed included.

11. Open web steel joists and steel lattice work shall be measured as a solid surface, both sides, based on the length and depth of the joist or lattice work.

12. Games lines, parking lines and the like shall be measured in metres.

13. Small tanks, pumps, motors and other equipment, valves and similar items shall be enumerated.

14. Letters and numerals shall be enumerated.

15. Test panels or mock-ups shall be enumerated.

16. Testing shall be given as an item.

17. Clean-up on completion shall be given as an item.

GENERALLY

1.   The section "General Rules" is to be read in conjunction with this Division.

2.   Unless otherwise stated, all items in this Division shall be enumerated.

10100 - VISUAL DISPLAY BOARDS

1.   Visual display boards shall be measured in the following categories:

     10110 - Chalkboards
     10115 - Markerboards
     10120 - Tackboard and visual aid boards
     10130 - Operable board units
     10140 - Display track assemblies
     10145 - Visual aid board units

2.   The description of the item shall include the method of fixing, and, where applicable, whether manually, mechanically or electrically operated.

10150 - COMPARTMENTS AND CUBICLES

1.   Compartments and cubicles shall be measured in the following categories:

     10160 - Metal toilet compartments
     10165 - Plastic laminate toilet compartments
     10170 - Plastic toilet compartments
     10175 - Particleboard toilet compartments
     10180 - Stone toilet compartments
     10185 - Shower and dressing compartments
     10190 - Cubicles

2.   Cubicle curtains and cubicle track and hardware shall be measured in Category 10190. Cubicle track may be measured in lineal metres, with bends, etc. enumerated.

3.   The description of the compartment or cubicle shall state whether the item is wall hung, ceiling hung or floor mounted.

4.   Toilet and bath accessories, which are to be provided by the manufacturer of the compartment or cubicle, shall be included in the description.

10200 - LOUVRES AND VENTS

1. Louvres and vents, which are not an integral part of the mechanical system, shall be measured in the following categories:

   10210 - Wall louvres
   10220 - Louvered equipment enclosures
   10225 - Door louvres
   10230 - Vents

10240 - GRILLES AND SCREENS

1. Exterior and interior screens, used for a variety of functions not limited to ventilation purposes, shall be measured in this category.

10260 - WALL AND CORNER GUARDS

1. Protective devices such as corner guards and bumper guards, unless of fabricated steel sections and plate, shall be measured in this category.

2. Continuous bumper guards shall be measured in metres; bends etc., shall be enumerated.

10270 - ACCESS FLOORING

1. Free standing access flooring including the floor finish, designed to form an underfloor cavity for mechanical or electrical distribution systems, shall be measured in this category.

2. Access flooring shall be measured in square metres.

10300 - FIREPLACES AND STOVES

1. Fireplaces and stoves shall be measured in the following categories:

   10305 - Manufactured fireplaces
   10310 - Fireplace specialties and accessories
   10320 - Stoves

2. Manufactured fireplace chimneys shall be measured in Category 10305, in lineal metres; bends, caps, etc., shall be enumerated.

3. Fireplace dampers, screens, doors, inserts, etc. shall be measured in Category 10310.

10340 - MANUFACTURED EXTERIOR SPECIALTIES

1. Clocks, cupolas, spires, steeples, weathervanes and the like shall be measured in this category.

10350 - FLAGPOLES

1. Automatic, ground-set and wall-mounted flagpoles shall be measured in this category, and shall include flags.

10400 - IDENTIFICATION DEVICES

1. Identification devices shall be measured in the following categories:

    10410 - Directories
    10420 - Plaques
    10430 - Exterior signage
    10440 - Interior signage

10450 - PEDESTRIAN CONTROL DEVICES

1. Detection and counting devices, portable posts and railings, rotary gates and turnstiles shall be measured in this category.

10500 - LOCKERS

1. Lockers shall be measured in this category.

10530 - PROTECTIVE COVERS

1. Awnings, canopies, car shelters, walkway coverings and the like shall be measured in this category.

10550 - POSTAL SPECIALTIES

1. Postal specialties shall be measured in this category.

10600 - PARTITIONS

1. Partitions shall be measured in the following categories:

    10605 - Wire mesh partitions
    10610 - Folding gates
    10615 - Demountable partitions
    10630 - Portable partitions, screens and panels
    10650 - Operable partitions

2. Wire mesh partitions shall be measured in metres stating the height.

3. Demountable partitions shall be measured in metres stating the height. Doors supplied by the partition manufacturer shall be measured as extra over the cost of the partition.

10670 - STORAGE SHELVING

1. Storage shelving shall be measured in this category.

2. Open, manufactured shelving for general storage, as opposed to specific items, shall be measured in this category.

10700 - EXTERIOR PROTECTION

1. Exterior protection shall be measured in the following categories:

    10705 - Exterior sun control devices
    10710 - Exterior shutters
    10715 - Storm panels
    10720 - Exterior louvres

10800 - TOILET AND BATH ACCESSORIES

1. Toilet and bath accessories shall be measured in the following categories:

    10810 - Toilet accessories
    10820 - Bath accessories
    10830 - Laundry accessories

10900 - WARDROBE AND CLOSET SPECIALTIES

1. Manufactured hat and coat racks, and other specialties for storage of clothing, shall be measured in this category.

GENERALLY

1. The section "General Rules" is to be read in conjunction with this Division.

2. All items in this Division, unless otherwise stated, shall be enumerated.

3. Many items in this Division are of a highly specialized nature, beyond the scope of normal building construction. A recommended method of measurement for such items has not been included herein.

11010 - MAINTENANCE EQUIPMENT

1. Floor and wall cleaning equipment, vacuum cleaning systems and window washing systems shall be measured in this category.

2. Within this category, guide and other rails shall be measured in metres.

11020 - SECURITY AND VAULT EQUIPMENT

1. Security and vault equipment shall be measured in this category.

11040 - ECCLESIASTICAL EQUIPMENT

1. Ecclesiastical equipment shall be measured in this category.

2. Chancel rails shall be measured in metres.

11050 - LIBRARY EQUIPMENT

1. Library equipment shall be measured in this category.

2. Shelving shall be measured in metres.

11060 - THEATRE AND STAGE EQUIPMENT

1. Acoustical shells, folding and portable stages and stage curtains shall be measured in this category.

11160 - LOADING DOCK EQUIPMENT

1. Loading dock equipment shall be measured in this category.

11170 - SOLID WASTE HANDLING EQUIPMENT

1. Garbage chutes shall be measured in this category.

2. Chutes shall be measured in metres. Access doors, control doors, collectors and the like shall be enumerated.

11400 - FOOD SERVICE EQUIPMENT

1. Food service equipment shall be measured in the following categories:

   11405 - Food storage equipment
   11410 - Food preparation equipment
   11420 - Food cooking equipment
   11425 - Hood and ventilation equipment
   11430 - Food dispensing equipment
   11435 - Ice machines
   11440 - Cleaning and disposal equipment

2. Within the above categories, continuous counter tops may be measured in metres or enumerated.

11450 - RESIDENTIAL EQUIPMENT

1. Residential appliances, residential kitchen equipment, retractable stairs and the like shall be measured in this category.

11600 - LABORATORY EQUIPMENT

1. Laboratory equipment shall be measured in this category. Continuous counter tops may be measured in metres or enumerated.

GENERALLY

1.   The section "General Rules" is to be read in conjunction with this Division.

2.   Unless otherwise stated, all items in this Division shall be enumerated.

12100 - ARTWORK

1.   Stained glass work shall be measured in this category.

12300 - MANUFACTURED CASEWORK

1.   Manufactured casework shall be measured in the following categories:

     12310 - Manufactured metal casework
     12320 - Manufactured wood casework
     12350 - Specialty casework

2.   The work in this Section applies to stock design cabinets and other casework units, manufactured from steel, wood and plastic laminate for a variety of uses. Site built, and site finished casework, shall be measured in Division 6.

12400 - FURNISHINGS AND ACCESSORIES

1.   Furnishings and accessories shall be measured in the following categories:

     12440 - Bath furnishings
     12480 - Rugs and mats
     12490 - Window treatments

2.   The description of blinds and shades shall include whether surface mounted, interior mounted or mounted between glass.

3.   Solar control film shall be measured in square metres.

4.   Track for hospital privacy curtains and the like shall be measured in metres.

5.   Draperies and curtains shall be enumerated by panels, the description shall include the percentage of fullness required.

6.   The description of stage, theatre or proscenium draperies shall include details of contour draping, control, traverse, rigging, counterweights, battens, tracks and all other required components.

12600 - MULTIPLE SEATING

1. Multiple seating shall be measured in the following categories:

    12610 - Fixed audience seating
    12630 - Stadium and arena seating
    12660 - Telescoping stands
    12670 - Pews and benches

12800 - INTERIOR PLANTS AND PLANTERS

1. Interior plants and planters shall be measured in the following categories:

    12810 - Interior live plants
    12830 - Interior planters
    12840 - Interior landscape accessories

GENERALLY

1. The section "General Rules" is to be read in conjunction with this Division.

2. Many items in this Division are of a highly specialized nature, beyond the scope of normal building construction. A recommended method of measurement for such items has not been included herein.

13030 - SPECIAL PURPOSE ROOMS

1. Special purpose rooms, including cold storage rooms, saunas and vaults shall be measured in this category.

2. Items in these categories may be enumerated or measured in detail in accordance with the method of measurement for the appropriate Divisions.

13090 - RADIATION PROTECTION

1. Radiation shielding components and structures for protection against radio frequency, e-ray and nuclear radiation shall be measured in this category.

2. Sub-surface materials, such as concrete, masonry etc. shall be measured in their appropriate Division.

3. Sheet materials shall generally be measured in square metres. Deductions shall be made for openings exceeding 0.50 m^2. All additional materials, to give protection at joints, corners, openings, screw holes etc. shall be measured in metres, or enumerated, as appropriate. Surface application to doors, frames, hatches, duct and pipe openings shall be enumerated.

4. Window and door frames, doors, louvres, pass throughs and other items specially fabricated for radiation applications shall be enumerated.

13150 - SWIMMING POOLS

1. Swimming pools shall normally be measured in detail in accordance with the method of measurement for the appropriate Divisions.

13170 - TUBS AND POOLS

1. Tubs and pools, including hot tubs and therapeutic pools, shall be enumerated and measured in this category.

13185 - KENNELS AND ANIMAL SHELTERS

1. Kennels and animal shelters shall normally be measured in detail in accordance with the method of measurement for the appropriate Divisions. Small individual items may be enumerated and included in this category.

13200 - STORAGE TANKS

1. Storage tanks shall be measured in this category.

2. Items in this category may be measured in detail in accordance with the method of measurement for the appropriate Divisions or, if small in size, may be enumerated.

13900 - FIRE SUPPRESSION

1. Fire suppression shall be measured in the following categories:

    13920 - Fire pumps
    13930 - Wet-pipe suppression sprinklers
    13935 - Dry-pipe fire suppression sprinklers
    13950 - Deluge fire suppression systems
    13975 - Standpipes and hoses

2. Pipework shall be measured in metres; pumps, fittings, valves, hangers, supports, fire stopping, hoses etc. shall be enumerated.

GENERALLY

1. The section "General Rules" is to be read in conjunction with this Division.

2. Many items in this Division are of a highly specialized nature, beyond the scope of normal building construction. A recommended method of measurement for such items has not been included herein.

3. All items in this Division, unless otherwise stated, shall be enumerated.

14100 - DUMBWAITERS

1. Dumbwaiters shall be measured in the following categories:

    14110 - Manual dumbwaiters
    14120 - Electric dumbwaiters
    14140 - Hydraulic dumbwaiters

14200 - ELEVATORS

1. Elevators shall be measured in the following categories:

    14210 - Electric traction elevators
    14240 - Hydraulic elevators

2. Within the above categories, passenger, service and freight elevators shall each be kept separate.

14300 - ESCALATORS AND MOVING WALKS

1. Escalators and moving walks shall be measured in this category.

14400 - LIFTS

1. Lifts shall be measured in the following categories:

    14410 - People lifts
    14420 - Wheelchair lifts
    14430 - Platform lifts
    14440 - Sidewalk lifts
    14450 - Vehicle lifts

14500 - MATERIAL HANDLING

1. Laundry, linen and refuse chutes shall be measured in this category:

    14560 - Chutes

2. Chutes may be enumerated, or measured in detail. Where measured in detail, straight lengths shall be measured in metres and all other items shall be enumerated.

GENERALLY

1. The section "General Rules" is to be read in conjunction with this Division.

2. Work within this Division shall commence, or terminate, 1.00 m from the outside face of the structure.

3. Pipework shall be measured in metres; fittings and valves shall be enumerated. No deduction in pipe lengths shall be made for fittings not exceeding 225 mm in diameter. Buried piping shall be so described.

4. With the exception of ductwork and mechanical insulation, all other items in this Division shall be enumerated. The method of measurement for ductwork and for mechanical insulation is detailed in the appropriate Section.

5. Items which are common to various Sections within this Division shall be measured separately with each Section. E.g. Hangers and supports, sleeves, fire stopping, roof flashings.

6. Vibration isolation materials shall be described with the item of equipment to which they relate.

CLASSIFICATIONS

1. The various classifications within the scope of "General Requirements" for this Division shall be measured and priced as "Items", unless a specific mode of measurement is recommended, in the following categories:

    1. Certificates and fees

        Include charges pertaining to fees, permits and licenses required for plumbing permit, Department of Labour, welding tests and other similar requirements.

    2. Liability and protection

        Include providing for errors, and protection of finishes.

    3. Record drawings

        Include the cost of producing as built drawings, when or where changes have been made from original drawings.

CLASSIFICATIONS (Continued)

1. 4. Shop drawings

Include processing and checking shop drawings.

5. Operating instructions and maintenance manuals

Include providing written operating instructions and maintenance manuals. Where required, shall also include the use of labour, fuel, water and other materials.

6. Contractor's shop

Include:

1. Providing, maintaining and removing all site offices, storage sheds, welfare accommodation and similar buildings, together with furniture, office equipment, services, and including all attendance thereon, heating and air conditioning if required.

.2 Installing and all charges for telephone and facsimile facilities.

7. Temporary and trial usage

If part of the system is used on a temporary or trial basis before completion, include adjusting, oiling, greasing and other similar requirements upon final completion.

8. Insurances

Include all contract and labour insurance, including Public Liability, Unemployment, Workmen's Compensation, Hospital, Vacation, Calamity and Marine.

9. Guarantee

Include a guarantee to cover defects in materials and workmanship for a specified period of time.

10. Preparation for painting

Include cleaning surfaces ready for painting and identification by Division 9.

CLASSIFICATIONS (Continued)

1.   11. Valve tags and charts

     Include providing valve tags and charts.

     12. Wall plates and access doors

     Include providing wall plates and access doors.

     13. Bases and supports

     Include steel bases or stands for mechanical equipment unless specifically
     measured with the item concerned. Include all miscellaneous steelwork
     related to this Division including that required for seismic bracing.

     14. Temporary plumbing

     Include all labour, material, permits and fees. Alternatively, it shall be
     measured in detail in accordance with the Method of Measurement for this
     Division.

     15. Testing

     Include all necessary labour and materials for testing each part of the system
     as required during the progress of the work and final testing upon completion.
     Alternatively testing may be measured under category 15950.

     16. Clean up

     Include the cost of cleaning up and disposing rubbish created by the operation
     of this Division

     17. Electrical wiring and starters

     Where the responsibility of this Division, cable, conduit and the like shall be
     measured in metres; all other work shall be enumerated.

     18. Personnel

     Include all managerial, technical and administrative personnel necessary to
     ensure efficient operation of the contract, together with all attendant expenses.

CLASSIFICATIONS (Continued)

1. 19. Layout

   Include all labour, material and instruments required for laying out the work of this Division.

   20. Hoisting

   Include hoisting major equipment of this Division which is beyond the capabilities of the General Contractor's hoisting equipment.

   21. Plant and equipment

   Include providing, installing and operating all tools and equipment used by this Division including fuel, maintenance, repairs and spare parts.

   22. Site visits

   Include the cost of all expenses incurred by supervisory staff on regular visits to the Works.

   23. Scaffolding

   Shall be enumerated by sections, giving height, and stating if special wheels are required.

   24. Premium time

   Include any special measures in respect of work involving overtime or shift work.

   25. Bonds

   Include Bid, Performance, Payment and Guarantee Bonds, Certified Cheques and Securities, stating the amount of the cover and whether payable by the Owner or Contractor.

   26. Travel expenses

   Include time lost in travel to and from Site and all fares payable under trade agreements and allowances for board and lodging.

CLASSIFICATIONS (Continued)

1. 27. Lost time

   Include time lost in reporting to Site when work is unable to be performed due to inclement weather as stated in Trade Agreement.

   28. Sales taxes and duties

   Include all sales taxes and duties in effect at the time of the Tender including any special exemptions or reimbursements.

   29. Cutting, patching and making good

   Unless measured in other Divisions, cutting, patching, canning, coring and making good shall be enumerated. The removal and replacement of ceilings and walls for access purposes shall be measured in square metres.

15080 - MECHANICAL INSULATION

1. Duct, equipment and piping insulation shall be measured in this category.

2. Piping insulation shall be measured in metres, and the purpose of the pipe stated. An allowance of 0.50 m of insulation shall be allowed for each fitting or valve.

3. Equipment insulation shall be measured in square metres, and the item of equipment stated.

4. Ductwork insulation shall be measured in square metres.

5. Prefabricated insulated panels shall be measured in square metres and the number of panels shall be stated.

6. An insulation media, for use with an underground distribution system, shall be measured in cubic metres, or by weight.

15100 - BUILDING SERVICES PIPING

1. Building services piping shall be measured in the following categories:

    15140 - Domestic water piping
    15150 - Sanitary waste and vent piping
    15160 - Storm drainage piping
    15170 - Swimming pool and fountain piping
    15180 - Heating and cooling piping
    15190 - Fuel piping

2. Valves, pumps, floor drains etc. shall be measured in the category to which they relate.

3. For less complex projects, all mechanical work relating to heating, ventilating and air conditioning may be measured in Category 15180; in this case it would contain items detailed in Sections 15100 - Building Services Piping, 15500 - Heat-generation Equipment, 15600 - Refrigeration Equipment, 15800 - Air Distribution and 15900 - HVAC Instrumentation and Controls.

15200 - PROCESS PIPING

1. Process piping shall be measured in the following categories:

    15210 - Process air and gas piping
    15220 - Process water and waste piping
    15230 - Industrial process piping

15300 - FIRE PROTECTION PIPING

1. Fire protection shall be measured either in this category or in Division 13 Category 13900.

15400 - PLUMBING FIXTURES AND EQUIPMENT

1. Plumbing fixtures and equipment shall be measured in the following categories:

    15410 - Plumbing fixtures
    15440 - Plumbing pumps
    15450 - Potable water storage tanks
    15480 - Domestic water heaters
    15490 - Pool and fountain equipment

15400 - PLUMBING FIXTURES AND EQUIPMENT (Continued)

2. Plumbing equipment shall include pumps, storage tanks, water heaters, etc.

3. Special systems shall include compressed air, fuel oil, natural gas, oxygen, vacuum, etc. Each system shall be measured separately under an appropriate heading.

15500 - HEAT-GENERATION EQUIPMENT

1. Heat-generation equipment shall be measured in the following categories:

> 15510 - Heating boilers and accessories
> 15520 - Feedwater equipment
> 15530 - Furnaces
> 15540 - Fuel-fired heaters
> 15550 - Breechings, chimneys and stacks

15600 - REFRIGERATION EQUIPMENT

1. Refrigeration equipment shall be measured in the following categories:

> 15610 - Refrigeration compressors
> 15620 - Packaged water chillers
> 15640 - Packaged cooling towers
> 15650 - Field-erected cooling towers
> 15660 - Liquid coolers and evaporative condensers
> 15670 - Refrigerant condensing units

15700 - HEATING, VENTILATING AND AIR CONDITIONING EQUIPMENT

1. Heating, ventilating and air conditioning equipment shall be measured in the following categories:

> 15710 - Heat exchangers
> 15720 - Air handling units
> 15730 - Unitary air conditioning equipment
> 15740 - Heat pumps
> 15750 - Humidity control equipment
> 15760 - Terminal heating and cooling units
> 15770 - Floor-heating and snow-melting equipment
> 15780 - Energy recovery equipment

15700 - HEATING, VENTILATING AND AIR CONDITIONING EQUIPMENT (Continued)

2.   All work within a boiler room, and within an equipment room, shall be so stated, and each shall be kept separate.

3.   An item of equipment which is to be assembled on site shall have the number of component parts enumerated.

15800 - AIR DISTRIBUTION

1.   Air distribution shall be measured in the following categories:

>   15810 - Ducts
>   15820 - Duct accessories
>   15830 - Fans
>   15840 - Air terminal units
>   15850 - Air outlets and inlets
>   15860 - Air cleaning devices

2.   Rectangular and circular ductwork shall be measured in metres and the resultant length converted into weight, as follows:

1.   Measure straight lengths between fittings and round up to next 0.25 m above, e.g. 2.30 m is rounded up to 2.50 m.

2.   Measure transitions to nearest 0.25 m and state the greater dimension at each end of the transition.

3.   Measure square elbows as the sum of the two long sides and round off to the nearest 0.25 m length; state the cross-sectional dimensions.

4.   Measure radius elbows as the sum of the tangential lengths and round off to the nearest 0.25 m length; state the cross-sectional dimensions.

5.   Measure "Y" fittings as the equivalent of two 45° radius elbows.

6.   Measure the length of tap-in tees, registers and diffuser collars and round off to the nearest 0.25 m length (minimum length 0.25 m); state the cross-sectional dimensions of the larger end.

7.   Measure 45° elbows at the straight length between the two extremes of the elbow and round off to the nearest 0.25 m length; state the cross-sectional dimensions.

15800 - AIR DISTRIBUTION (Continued)

2.   8.   Measure offsets as the equivalent of two 45° elbows.

9.   Measure duct ends as the length of the lesser dimension of the end and round off to the nearest 0.25 m.

10.   Enumerate the number of fittings in order to calculate the "fitting to duct length" ratio for pricing purposes.

11.   To the total weight of duct (the conversion of length to weight shall be obtained from appropriate tables) add the following:

1.   Sheet metal ducts - 20% to cover seams, joints, cleats, hangers, sealants and waste.

2.   Fibreglass ducts - 15% to cover waste <u>plus</u> 7 kg per 10 m^2 to cover hangers and supports.

3.   Duct liners - 15% to cover waste.

4.   Welded black iron ducts - 30% to cover seams, joints, cleats, hangers, sealants and waste.

3.   Spiral ductwork shall be measured in metres. All fittings shall be enumerated.

4.   Prefabricated insulated panels shall be measured in square metres and the number of panels shall be stated. This work may be measured in category 15080.

15900 - HVAC INSTRUMENTATION AND CONTROLS

1. HVAC instrumentation and controls shall be measured in the following categories:

    15905 - HVAC instrumentation
    15910 - Direct digital controls
    15915 - Electric and electronic controls
    15920 - Pneumatic controls
    15925 - Pneumatic and electric controls
    15930 - Self-powered controls
    15935 - Building systems controls

15950 - TESTING, ADJUSTING AND BALANCING

1. Testing, adjusting and balancing, where not included under General Requirements, shall be given as items in this category.

GENERALLY

1. The section "General Rules" is to be read in conjunction with this Division.

2. Cable, wire, ducts, raceways, conduits, etc. shall be measured in metres; bends, fittings, supports, fastenings and all other items in this Division shall be enumerated.

3. Items which are common to various Sections within this Division shall be measured separately with each Section. E.g. Hangers and supports, sleeves, fire stopping, roof flashings.

CLASSIFICATIONS

1. The various classifications within the scope of "General Requirements" for this Division shall be measured and priced as "Items", unless a specific mode of measurement is recommended, in the following categories:

    1. Certificates and fees

        Include charges pertaining to fees, permits and licenses required for electrical permit, Department of Labour, resistance tests and other similar requirements.

    2. Liability and protection

        Include providing for errors, and protection of finishes.

    3. Record drawings

        Include the cost of producing as built drawings, when or where changes have been made from original drawings.

    4. Shop drawings

        Include processing and checking shop drawings.

    5. Operating instructions and maintenance manuals

        Include providing written operating instructions and maintenance manuals. Where required, shall also include the use of labour, fuel, water and other materials.

CLASSIFICATIONS (Continued)

1. 6. Contractor's shop

   Include:

   1. Providing, maintaining and removing all site offices, storage sheds, welfare accommodation and similar buildings, together with furniture, office equipment, services, and including all attendance thereon, heating and air conditioning if required.

   2. Installing and all charges for telephone and facsimile facilities.

   7. Temporary and trial usage

   Include, if part of the system is used on a temporary or trial basis, adjusting, cleaning and other similar requirements upon final completion.

   8. Insurances

   Include all contract and labour insurances, including Public Liability, Unemployment, Workmen's Compensation, Hospital, Vacation, Calamity and Marine.

   9. Guarantee

   Include a guarantee to cover defects in materials and workmanship for a specified period of time.

   10. Identification tags

   Include providing identification tags.

   11. Bases and supports

   Include steel bases or stands for electrical equipment unless specifically measured with the item concerned. Shall also include all miscellaneous steelwork related to this Division including that required for seismic bracing.

   12. Testing

   Include all necessary labour and materials for testing each part of the system as required during the progress of the work and final testing upon completion.

CLASSIFICATIONS (Continued)

1. 13. Clean up

    Include the cost of cleaning up and disposing rubbish created by the operation of this Division.

    14. Personnel

    Include all managerial, technical and administrative personnel necessary to ensure efficient operation of the contract, together with all attendant expenses.

    15. Layout

    Include all labour, material and instruments required for laying out the work of this Division.

    16. Hoisting

    Include hoisting major equipment of this Division which is beyond the capabilities of the General Contractor's hoisting equipment.

    17. Plant and equipment

    Include providing, installing and operating all tools and equipment used by this Division including fuel, maintenance, repairs and spare parts.

    18. Site visits

    Include the cost of all expenses incurred by supervisory staff on regular visits to the Works.

    19. Scaffolding

    Shall be enumerated by sections, giving height, and stating if special wheels are required.

    20. Premium time

    Include any special measures in respect of work involving overtime or shift work.

CLASSIFICATIONS (Continued)

1. 21. Bonds

   Include Bid, Performance, Payment and Guarantee Bonds, Certified Cheques and Securities, stating the amount of the cover and whether payable by the Owner or Contractor.

   22. Travel expenses

   Include time lost in travel to and from the Site and all fares payable under trade agreements and allowances for board and lodging.

   23. Lost time

   Include time lost in reporting to Site when work is unable to be performed due to inclement weather as stated in Trade Agreement.

   24. Sales taxes and duties

   Include all sales taxes and duties in effect at the time of the Tender including any special exemptions or reimbursements.

   25. Cutting, patching and making good

   Unless measured in other Divisions, cutting, patching, canning, coring and making good shall be enumerated. The removal and replacement of ceilings and walls for access purposes shall be measured in square metres.

16100 - WIRING METHODS

1. Wiring etc. shall be measured in the following categories:

   16120 - Conductors and cables
   16130 - Raceways and boxes
   16140 - Wiring devices
   16150 - Wiring connections

16200 - ELECTRICAL POWER

1.   Electrical power shall be measured in the following categories:

      16210 - Electrical utility services
      16220 - Motors and generators
      16230 - Generator assemblies
      16240 - Battery equipment
      16260 - Static power converters
      16270 - Transformers
      16280 - Power filters and conditioners
      16290 - Power measurement and control

16300 - TRANSMISSION AND DISTRIBUTION

1.   Transmission and distribution shall be measured in the following categories:

      16310 - Transmission and distribution accessories
      16320 - High-voltage switching and protection
      16330 - Medium-voltage switching and protection
      16340 - Medium-voltage switching and protection assemblies
      16360 - Unit substations

16400 - LOW-VOLTAGE DISTRIBUTION

1.   Low-voltage distribution shall be measured in the following categories:

      16410 - Enclosed switches and circuit breakers
      16420 - Enclosed controllers
      16430 - Low-voltage switchgear
      16440 - Switchboards, panelboards and control centres
      16450 - Enclosed bus assemblies
      16460 - Low-voltage transformers
      16470 - Power distribution units

16500 - LIGHTING

1.   Lighting shall be measured in the following categories:

        16510 - Interior luminaires
        16520 - Exterior luminaires
        16530 - Emergency lighting
        16550 - Special purpose lighting
        16570 - Dimming control
        16580 - Lighting accessories

16700 - COMMUNICATIONS

1.   Communications shall be measured in the following categories:

        16710 - Communications circuits
        16720 - Telephone and intercommunication equipment
        16740 - Communications and data processing equipment
        16770 - Cable transmission and reception equipment
        16780 - Broadcast transmission and reception equipment
        16790 - Microwave transmission and reception equipment,

16800 - SOUND AND VIDEO

1.   Sound and video shall be measured in the following categories:

        16810 - Sound and video circuits
        16820 - Sound reinforcement

Method of Measurement of Construction Works

Seventh Edition

Imperial Version

GENERALLY

1. The section "General Rules" is to be read in conjunction with this Division.

2. The various classifications within the scope of this Division shall be measured and priced as "Items", (unless a specific mode of measurement is recommended).

01100 - SUMMARY

1. 01100 - Summary of work

   1. Personnel

      Include all managerial, technical and administrative personnel (such as project manager, superintendent, foreman, engineer, timekeeper, first-aid attendant, etc.) necessary to ensure the efficient operation of the project, together with attendant expenses.

   2. Mobilization

      Include all costs incurred for moving onto the site, mobilization and set-up; and moving out at completion of project.

   3. Rental of adjacent property

      Include the rental of adjacent property, including restoration of any damage.

   4. Rental of parking meters, sidewalks and land

      Include all charges in connection with fees and licences for rental of parking meters, sidewalks and land.

   5. Camp

      Include the cost of establishing a camp for the workforce, maintenance, provisions and supplies, and removing at completion of the project.

   6. Bonds

      Include the cost of Bid, Performance, Labour and Material Payment and Guarantee Bonds, Certified Cheques and Securities, as specified.

01100 - SUMMARY (Continued)

1.   01100 - Summary of work (Continued)

7.   Insurances

Include the cost of all insurances specified for the project, including Demolition, All Risk and Public Liability.

8.   Finances

Include the cost of any interim financing

01300 - ADMINISTRATIVE REQUIREMENTS

1.   01300 - Project Management and Coordination

1.   Head office travel

Include all expenses incurred by supervisory personnel on regular visits to the site.

2.   01330 - Submittal procedures

1.   Construction photographs

Include the cost of site photographs if required by the Specification.

01400 - QUALITY REQUIREMENTS

1.   01410 - Regulatory requirements

1.   Permanent utility connections

Include any charges for the permanent connection of hydro, water, gas, sanitary and storm sewers, if not included in another Division.

2.   Travel expenses

Include time lost in travel to and from site, travel allowances payable under trade agreements, and allowances for board and lodging.

01400 - QUALITY REQUIREMENTS (Continued)

1. 01410 - Regulatory requirements (Continued)

    3. Miscellaneous permits

       Include all miscellaneous permits pertaining to the project, including utility inspection charges, sidewalk and road repairs, and damage deposits.

    4. Premium time

       Include the cost of premium time to meet schedule requirements stipulated in the tender documents.

    5. Permits

       Include the cost of the Building Permit, Development Permit and Development Cost Charges.

    6. Warranty programs

       Include the cost of complying with all required warranty programs.

    7. Labour rate increase

       Include all labour rate increases that may occur during the duration of the project.

    8. Payroll levies

       Include all payment levies; e.g. holiday pay, U.I.C., C.P.P., union dues, apprenticeship training funds and the like, if not included in the labour rates used for pricing.

    9. Sales taxes

       Include all applicable Provincial Sales Taxes and Federal dues.

    10. Goods and Services Tax

        Include the Goods and Services Tax, noting any special exemptions or reductions to the current tax rate.

01400 - QUALITY REQUIREMENTS (Continued)

2.　01450 - Quality control

   1.　Material testing

   Include the cost of testing concrete, gravel or backfill compaction, asphalt and any other testing required by the Specification, unless paid for by the Owner.

01500 - TEMPORARY FACILITIES AND CONTROL

1.　Provide, erect, operate, maintain and remove temporary facilities and controls for use on site during construction, including all necessary operators, labour and attendance, fuel, maintenance, repairs, spare parts, moving to and from site, loading and unloading, charges and rentals.

2.　01510 - Temporary utilities

   1.　Electricity
   2.　Fire protection
   3.　Fuel oil
   4.　Heating, cooling and ventilating
   5.　Lighting
   6.　Natural gas
   7.　Telephone
   8.　Water
   9.　Sewers

3.　01520 - Construction facilities

   Include furniture, office equipment, telephone, facsimile machine and supplies.

   1.　Field offices and sheds
   2.　First aid
   3.　Sanitary facilities
   4.　Fire protection including portable fire extinguishers and fire hoses

4.　01530 - Temporary construction

   1.　Bridges
   2.　Decking
   3.　Ramps

01500 - TEMPORARY FACILITIES AND CONTROL (Continued)

5. 01540 - Temporary construction aids

    1. Construction elevators, hoists and cranes (include bases)
    2. Scaffolding and platforms
    3. Swing staging
    4. Wind bracing (if not included elsewhere in the Specification)
    5. Stairs and ladders
    6. Garbage and disposal chutes
    7. Pumping and other equipment (if not priced under trade operations)
    8. Small tools
    9. Winter protection (include tarpaulins, heaters, temporary enclosures, insulation mats, heated concrete, snow and ice removal)

6. 01550 - Vehicular access and parking

    1. Access roads (measurements shall be in feet)
    2. Parking and storage areas (measurements shall be in square feet)
    3. Traffic control

7. 01560 - Temporary barriers and enclosures

    Provide for protection of occupants, the general public or existing spaces, including:

    1. Barricades
    2. Dust barriers and temporary partitions
    3. Fences
    4. Protective walkways (include lighting)
    5. Tree and plant protection
    6. Planking for the protection of trenches and pits (include   safety lamps and warning signs)
    7. Shoring/underpinning (unless included in other Divisions as part of the permanent work)
    8. Railings to perimeters of floors and roofs and at openings as required to meet Workers Compensation Board regulations

    Include painting where required. Measurements shall be in feet, square feet, or enumerated as appropriate.

01500 - TEMPORARY FACILITIES AND CONTROL (Continued)

8. 01570 - Temporary controls

    1. Temporary site drainage, including pumping any temporary ditches, sumps, catch-basins and shoring the face of excavations.
    2. Watchman or security services
    3. Flagman or signalman

9. 01580 - Project identification

    1. Project signs

01700 - EXECUTION REQUIREMENTS

1. 01720 - Field engineering

    1. Providing labour, materials and instruments for the proper layout out of the works.

    2. Include for the services and fees of a professional land surveyor.

2. 01740 - Cleaning

    1. Final cleaning

        Include removing all temporary or protective coverings; washing and final polishing of all windows and other glass surfaces including the inside of unsealed double glazing units, floor and wall tiles, sheet goods and the like; vacuuming carpets; cleaning, oiling and adjusting hardware. Measurements may be in square feet, or as an item.

    2. Progress cleaning

    3. Site maintenance

        Include keeping the site and building free from all rubbish, provision of disposal container and dumping charges.

3. 01760 - Protecting installed construction

        Provide and maintain temporary coverings to floors and finished work and remove on completion. Measurements shall be in square feet.

01800 - FACILITY OPERATION

1.   01830 - Operation and maintenance

   1.   Maintenance

   Include the cost of any required maintenance of the building, equipment and systems and the site development work after installation and during subsequent construction.

   Where specifically required, include the cost of any required maintenance after substantial completion.

GENERALLY

1.   The section "General Rules" is to be read in conjunction with this Division.

02100 - SITE REMEDIATION

1.   Site remediation shall be measured in the following categories:

> 02105 - Chemical sampling and analysis
> 02110 - Excavation, removal and handling of hazardous material
> 02115 - Underground storage tank removal
> 02120 - Off-site transportation and disposal
> 02130 - Site decontamination
> 02150 - Hazardous waste recovery processes
> 02160 - Physical treatment
> 02170 - Chemical treatment
> 02180 - Thermal processes
> 02190 - Biological processes

2.   02105 - Chemical sampling and analysis shall be stated as an item.

3.   02110 - Hazardous material

   1.   The removal of hazardous material, such as asbestos, requires the preparation of the work area, including providing a negative air pressure and the provision of a decontamination unit. The hazardous material may be covered by a finish material, such as drywall, or ceiling tile, which itself will be contaminated, and must be removed prior to removing the hazardous material.

   2.   Temporary floor covering, and taping and sealing door and window openings, shall each be measured separately in square feet. The provision of an air pump, including the replacement of filters, shall be enumerated. The setting up, maintenance and removal of a decontamination unit shall be enumerated.

   3.   The removal of the covering material shall be measured in square feet.

   4.   The removal of hazardous material shall be measured as follows:

      1.   From floors, walls and ceilings - in square feet
      2.   From pipes - in feet
      3.   From boilers, and other items of equipment - enumerated.

02100 - SITE REMEDIATION (Continued)

5. The disposal of hazardous material and contaminated waste shall be given as an item.

4. 02120 - Underground storage tank removal shall be enumerated.

5. 02130 - Site decontamination shall be measured in square feet.

6. 02160 - 02190 - Soil decontamination shall be measured in cubic yards.

02200 - SITE PREPARATION

1. Site preparation shall be measured in the following categories;

    02220 - Site demolition
    02230 - Site clearing
    02240 - Dewatering
    02250 - Shoring and underpinning
    02260 - Excavation support and protection

2. 02220 - Site demolition

    1. General principles

        1. Any assumptions made in the preparation of the measurement shall be so stated.

        2. Material to be salvaged, either for reuse or for handing over   to   the Owner, shall be so described.

        3. General protection shall not be measured. Special protection, where specified, either on a permanent or temporary basis, shall be measured in accordance with the relevant Divisions of this Method of Measurement.

        4. The removal of demolished items from site, and their final disposal shall be measured separately.

        5. Special insurance requirements shall be stated in Division 1.

02200 - SITE PREPARATION (Continued)

2.   02220 - Site demolition (Continued)

2.   Building demolition

1.   Structures to be completely demolished shall be enumerated and described in general terms, giving the type of structure and building systems, and the overall dimensions.

3.   Selective demolition

1.   Parts of structures to be demolished shall be measured in detail within this Section. No deductions shall be made from the measurements of openings for doors, windows, skylights and the like.

2.   Temporary shoring, where required, shall be stated with the item of demolition.

3.   Work relating to making good shall be measured in accordance with the relevant Divisions of this Method of Measurement.

4.   Demolition of concrete foundations, columns, beams, and staircases shall be measured in cubic yards and described as reinforced or unreinforced.

5.   Demolition of roads, floors, walls and roofs shall be measured in square yards or square feet. Applied finishings shall be described.

6.   Demolition of structural steel columns, beams, joists, etc. shall each be separately enumerated.

7.   Demolition of doors, windows, millwork, specialties, etc. shall be enumerated.

8.   Demolition of suspended ceilings shall be measured in square yards.

9.   Cutting or enlarging openings in walls, floors and roofs shall be enumerated.

10. Demolition of conveying systems and mechanical and electrical services shall be measured in the same units used for installation, as described in the relevant Divisions in this Method of Measurement.

02200 - SITE PREPARATION (Continued)

2.　02220 - Site demolition (Continued)

   3.　Selective demolition (Continued)

      11.　Disconnecting and capping services and utilities shall be enumerated.

3.　02230 - Site clearing

   1.　An item of "Site clearing" shall be measured in square yards to cover the removal of shrubs, trees (not exceeding 1 foot girth) and other vegetable matter.

   2.　Trees to be removed shall be enumerated and grouped according to size (measured 5 feet above ground level) as follows:

      Exceeding 1 foot but not exceeding 3 feet girth
      Exceeding 3 feet but not exceeding 6 feet girth
      Exceeding 6 feet but not exceeding 9 feet girth

      The item shall be deemed to include cutting down, grubbing up roots and burning or removing material from site.

   3.　Stripping and disposal of top soil (either off site or stored on site for later reuse in landscaping) shall be measured ("bank measure") in cubic yards.

   4.　The demolition of fences, walls and the like shall be measured in yards; the items shall be deemed to include the removal of foundations and disposal off site.

4.　02240 - Dewatering

   1.　The removal of subsurface water for preparation of foundations, pipe bedding and other work shall be given as an item.

5.　02250 - Shoring and underpinning

   1.　When shoring is specifically ordered, it shall be measured in square yards to both sides of trenches and to the faces of other excavations.

   2.　The length of the wall to be supported in underpinning shall be measured in yards. Details of the wall shall include the height, number of floors and type of foundation.

02200 - SITE PREPARATION (Continued)

    6.   02260 - Excavation support and protection

         1.   Soil and rock anchors shall be enumerated in this category.

02300 - EARTHWORK

    1.   General principles

         1.   Earthwork shall be measured in the following categories:

                02310 - Grading
                02315 - Excavation and fill
                02335 - Subgrade and roadbed
                02340 - Soil stabilization
                02370 - Erosion and sedimentation control

         2.   Earthwork shall be measured in cubic yards unless otherwise stated.

         3.   Excavation and fill shall be measured "bank measure".

         4.   The type of material to be excavated shall be stated. Any restrictions on blasting, where the excavation is in rock, shale or hardpan, shall be stated.

         5.   Allowances for working space for temporary shoring, the erection and removal of formwork, the application of waterproofing or the laying of pipes shall be as follows:

             1.   To footing – 6 inches from face of footing or 2 feet from face of wall above, whichever is greater.

             2.   To trench and face of mass excavation – 2 feet from face of wall or 6 inches from face of footing below, whichever is greater.

             3.   To trenches for pipes not exceeding 12 inches in diameter – pipe diameter plus 1 foot on each side of the pipe.

             4.   To trenches for pipes exceeding 12 inches in diameter – pipe diameter plus 2 feet on each side of the pipe.

             Where special circumstances require the provision of more working space than indicated above, the assumed dimensions of the working space shall be stated.

02300 - EARTHWORK (Continued)

1. General principles (Continued)

    5. (Continued)

        Alternatively, if customary in the particular location, working space shall not be measured and this shall be so stated.

    6. Unless permanent shoring is measured, additional excavation shall be measured to permit the following angles of repose:

Rock, shale and hardpan	nil
Stiff clay	4:1
Clay	3:1
Earth	2:1
Sand	1:1

    7. Temporary shoring of excavation shall not be measured. Permanent shoring or other form of protection shall be measured in square feet to all faces to be upheld.

    8. All excavation items shall be deemed to include dumping on site in spoil heaps. An item shall be measured for disposal off site for material surplus to requirements. Fill from borrow pits on site, and imported fill, shall be measured separately.

2. 02310 - Grading

    1. Grading shall be measured in square yards.

3. 02315 - Excavation and fill

    1. Excavating, mass fill and backfill shall be classified as follows:

        1. Bulk work to reduce or make up levels
        2. Basements
        3. Trenches
        4. Column bases and pits
        5. Ducts and miscellaneous
        6. Shafts, manholes and wells
        7. Trenches for the mechanical and electrical trades
        8. Work required to be performed by hand or by some other specified means.

02300 - EARTHWORK (Continued)

3.   02315 - Excavation and fill (Continued)

    2.   Trimming and grading bottoms or sides of excavation shall not be measured unless they are to be used as formwork.

4.   02335 - Subgrade and roadbed

    1.   Preparation of subgrades and roadbeds shall be measured in square yards.

5.   02340 - Soil stabilization

    1.   Soil stabilization shall be measured in square yards.

6.   02370 - Erosion and sedimentary control

    1.   Paving, blankets and mats shall be measured in square yards.

    2.   Gabions, riprap and the like shall be measured in cubic yards.

    3.   Water course and slope erosion protection shall be measured in yards.

02400 - TUNNELING, BORING AND JACKING

1.   Tunnel excavation etc. shall be measured in this category. The general principles and method of measurement contained in other clauses in this Division shall apply.

02450 - FOUNDATION AND LOAD-BEARING ELEMENTS

1.   General principles

    1.   Foundation and load-bearing elements shall be measured in the following categories:

        02455 - Driven piles
        02465 - Bored piles
        02475 - Caissons
        02490 - Anchors

    2.   Piles shall be measured in feet, from tip to cut-off level, unless otherwise stated.

02450 - FOUNDATION AND LOAD-BEARING ELEMENTS (Continued)

1. General principles (Continued)

    3. All available information relating to the site and sub-surface conditions shall be given with the measurements of piling.

    4. Restrictions relating to the level from which piling may be driven shall be stated.

    5. Piling which is to be carried out in water or under any limiting conditions relating to access or methods shall be measured separately, stating the restrictions.

    6. The cost of all record keeping shall be included in the piling rate.

    7. Anchors shall be enumerated.

2. 02455 - Driven piles

    1. Piling shall be classified as follows:

        1. Cast-in-place concrete piles
        2. Composite piles
        3. Concrete displacement piles
        4. Concrete filled steel piles
        5. Precast concrete piles
        6. Prestressed concrete piles
        7. Sheet piles
        8. Timber piles

    2. Within the above classifications bearing piles shall be grouped by lengths in increments of 3 feet and the number of piles in each grouping shall be stated.

    3. Battered piles shall be measured separately, stating the angle of batter.

    4. Splicing and lengthening piles, where required, shall be enumerated, stating the additional length.

    5. Sheet piles shall be measured in square feet on the net (undeveloped) areas to be supported. The rates shall include permanent and temporary supports and cutting.

02450 - FOUNDATION AND LOAD-BEARING ELEMENTS (Continued)

2. 02455 - Driven piles (Continued)

    6. Rates for concrete filled steel piles shall include excavation and filling within the casing.

    7. Test piling shall be measured separately. Setting up over each pile, and testing, shall be enumerated.

    8. Piling to be extracted shall be measured in accordance with the above principles. Disposal of the extracted material shall be described.

3. 02465 - Bored piles

    1. Piling shall be classified as follows:

        1. Auger cast group piles
        2. Bored and belled concrete piles
        3. Bored and socketed piles
        4. Bored friction concrete piles
        5. Drilled caissons
        6. Uncased cast-in-place concrete piles

    2. The method of measurement described above for 02455 - Driven piles shall apply, as applicable, to bored piles.

    3. The expansion or other treatment of the base of the pile, where required, is to be included in the description of the pile.

4. 02475 - Caissons

    1. Caissons shall be measured in accordance with the rules for the relevant item, i.e. excavation, concrete, etc., set out in this Method of Measurement.

02500 - UTILITY SERVICES

1. Utility services shall be measured in the following categories:

    02510 - Water distribution
    02520 - Wells
    02530 - Sanitary sewage
    02540 - Septic tank systems
    02550 - Piped energy distribution
    02580 - Electrical and communication structures

2. Utility services shall be measured in this Division up to 3 feet from the outside face of the structure.

3. Pipes, culverts and ducts shall be measured in feet; no deduction shall be made in pipe lengths for fittings not exceeding 9 inches in diameter. Fittings, valves, hydrants, valve boxes, pumps, cisterns, thrust and anchor blocks, drainage bends, junctions, connections and the like, catch-basins, sump pits, manholes, pull boxes etc., shall be enumerated.

4. Drilling or jetting wells shall be measured in feet. Disinfecting water mains shall be stated as an item.

5. Connection charges shall be stated as an item.

6. Septic and similar interceptor tanks, concrete slabs etc. shall be measured in accordance with the rules for the relevant items in this Method of Measurement.

02600 - DRAINAGE AND CONTAINMENT

1. Drainage and containment shall be measured in the following categories:

    02610 - Pipe culverts
    02620 - Subdrainage
    02630 - Storm drainage
    02640 - Culverts and manufactured construction
    02660 - Ponds and reservoirs

2. Drainage shall be measured in this Division up to 3 feet from the outside face of the structure.

02600 - DRAINAGE AND CONTAINMENT (Continued)

3. Pipe culverts and drainage pipes shall be measured in feet; no deduction shall be made in pipe lengths for bends, junctions etc. not exceeding 9 inches in diameter. Bends, junctions, connections, catch-basins, sump pits, manholes shall be enumerated.

4. Connection charges shall be stated as an item.

5. Interceptor tanks, concrete slabs, manufactured culverts, ponds, reservoirs, etc. shall be measured in accordance with the rules for the relevant items in this Method of Measurement.

02700 - BASES, BALLASTS, PAVEMENTS AND APPURTENANCES

1. Bases, ballasts, pavements and appurtenances shall be measured in the following categories:

    02710 - Bound base courses
    02720 - Unbound base courses and ballasts
    02730 - Aggregate surfacing
    02740 - Flexible paving
    02750 - Rigid pavement
    02760 - Paving specialties
    02770 - Curbs and gutters
    02775 - Sidewalks
    02780 - Unit pavers
    02785 - Flexible pavement coating and micro-sealing
    02790 - Athletic and recreational surfaces
    02795 - Porous pavement

2. Bound and unbound base courses and ballasts shall be measured in cubic yards and shall include all rolling and compacting.

3. Surfacing, paving and sidewalks shall be measured in square yards; curbs and gutters shall be measured in yards. Cutting back the edge of existing pavement, where specifically required, shall be measured in yards. Pavement marking shall be measured in yards, or shall be enumerated, as appropriate.

4. Paving and surfacing to slopes exceeding 30° from the horizontal shall be so described.

02800 - SITE IMPROVEMENTS AND AMENITIES

1. Site improvements and amenities shall be measured in the following categories:

    02810 - Irrigation system
    02815 - Fountains
    02820 - Fences and gates
    02830 - Retaining walls
    02840 - Walk, road and parking appurtenances
    02870 - Site furnishings
    02875 - Site and street shelters
    02880 - Play field equipment and structures
    02890 - Traffic signs and signals

2. Pipes in irrigation systems shall be measured in feet. Bends, junctions, connections etc. shall be deemed to be included in the measurement of the pipe. Sprinklers, valves, controls etc. shall be enumerated.

3. Fences, guard rails, barriers etc. shall be measured in feet. Gates shall be enumerated. Post holes and concrete, or other filling, shall be enumerated.

4. Other manufactured items within these categories shall be enumerated, unless another form of measurement is appropriate for a specific item. Contractor built items shall be measured in accordance with the rules for the relevant material in this Method of Measurement.

02900 - PLANTING

1. Planting shall be measured in the following categories:

    02905 - Transplanting
    02910 - Plant preparation
    02920 - Lawns and grasses
    02930 - Exterior plants
    02935 - Plant maintenance
    02945 - Planting accessories

2. Topsoil, seeding, sodding, other surface treatments and maintenance shall be measured in square yards. Work carried out to slopes exceeding 30° from the horizontal shall be so described.

3. Ground covers, plants, shrubs and trees shall be enumerated.

4. Landscape edging shall be measured in feet, tree grates shall be enumerated.

GENERALLY

1. The section "General Rules" is to be read in conjunction with this Division

2. The major items in this Division shall be measured in the following units unless otherwise stated:

    1. formwork in square feet
    2. reinforcing steel in pounds and welded wire fabric in square feet
    3. concrete in cubic yards.

03100 - CONCRETE FORMS AND ACCESSORIES

1. Concrete forms and accessories shall be measured in the following categories:

    03110 - Structural cast-in-place concrete forms
    03120 - Architectural cast-in-place concrete forms
    03130 - Permanent forms
    03150 - Concrete accessories

2. Formwork shall be measured to the actual surface in contact with the concrete. The function of the concrete shall be described, e.g. footing, column, wall.

3. No deductions shall be made for openings not exceeding 100 square feet, nor for the intersection of beams, slab bands, walls etc.

4. All temporary supports, bracing, strutting, re-shoring, scaffolding, guard rails, walkways and general falsework shall form part of the items of work to which they relate, and shall not be measured separately.

5. All form ties of whatever type, cutting back ties and grouting holes, form oil, fixings, plywood, studs, wailers, stripping, cleaning, oiling, lifting, transporting and any other labour or material necessary for the construction of the concrete formwork shall form part of the item to which they relate, and shall not be measured separately.

6. Notching and boring formwork shall not be measured.

7. Formwork to concrete surfaces not exceeding 8 inches wide or deep shall be measured in feet.

8. Formwork to circular columns shall be measured in feet.

03100 - CONCRETE FORMS AND ACCESSORIES (Continued)

9. Designed indents, rebates, fillets, coves, arrises, mouldings, block-outs, etc., which are attached to the face of the formwork, shall be measured in feet. Such items not exceeding 1 foot in length shall be enumerated.

10. Small items attached to formwork, such as inserts, anchors, plates, pipe cones, etc., shall be enumerated.

11. Items which are at the discretion of the contractor, such as pour strips, shall not be measured.

12. Formwork which is single sided shall be so described.

13. Formwork to confined spaces shall be kept separate.

14. Scribing formwork to rock face or profile shall be measured in feet.

15. Formwork to walls and columns exceeding 10 feet in height shall be measured separately in 5 feet increments.

16. Formwork to underside of suspended slabs, to soffits of slab bands, column heads, drop panels and to sides and soffits of beams, shall each be grouped according to height. Where over 10 feet high, the height shall be stated in increments of 5 feet.

17. Anchors and inserts shall be enumerated; expansion and contraction joints, waterstops and the like shall be measured in feet.

03200 - CONCRETE REINFORCEMENT

1. Concrete reinforcement shall be measured in the following categories:

    03210 - Reinforcing steel
    03220 - Welded wire fabric
    03230 - Stressing tendons
    03250 - Post tensioning

2. Reinforcing steel shall be classified by size, each size being given separately. The full length including laps, bends and hooks shall be measured. Tying wire, distance blocks and ordinary spacers shall be deemed to be included, and the weight of such items shall not be added to the weight of the reinforcing steel.

03200 - CONCRETE REINFORCEMENT (Continued)

3.   Within each size classification main reinforcing steel shall be further classified as straight, or with up to four bends per bar. Stirrups and links shall be so described and shall be deemed to include up to five bends per bar. Reinforcing steel which falls outside the number of bends in these categories shall be separately described.

4.   Reinforcing steel in lengths exceeding 40 feet shall be kept separate.

5.   Welded wire fabric shall be measured as the area covered. No deduction shall be made for voids not exceeding 10 square feet. Tying wire and distance blocks shall be deemed to be included.

6.   Stressing tendons for post-tensioned concrete shall be measured with category 03380.

03300 - CAST-IN-PLACE CONCRETE

1.   Cast-in-place concrete shall be measured in the following categories:

     03310 - Structural concrete
     03330 - Architectural concrete
     03340 - Low density concrete
     03350 - Concrete finishing
     03360 - Concrete finishes
     03370 - Specially placed concrete
     03380 - Post-tensioned concrete
     03390 - Concrete curing

2.   No deduction shall be made for concrete displaced by other materials cast into the concrete, nor for openings not exceeding 1 cubic foot in volume.

3.   Concrete that, by reason of its location or nature, must be pumped or continuously poured, or specifically compacted or vibrated, shall be so described.

4.   Integral admixtures to concrete shall be measured in cubic yards as extra over the cost of concrete to be so treated.

5.   Concrete finishing, concrete finishes and concrete curing shall be measured in square yards.

03300 - CAST-IN-PLACE CONCRETE (Continued)

6.   All work associated with post-tensioned concrete shall be measured under a separate heading, with the constituent parts measured in accordance with the foregoing principles. Cables which are to be tensioned, and tube ducts shall be measured in feet. Separate items shall be given for initial tensioning, for pressure grouting, and for additional tensioning if required. Grouting prestressing tendons shall be enumerated.

03400 - PRECAST CONCRETE

1.   Precast concrete shall be measured in the following categories:

        03410 - Plant-precast structural concrete
        03420 - Plant-precast structural post-tensioned concrete
        03430 - Site-precast structural concrete
        03450 - Plant-precast architectural concrete
        03460 - Site-precast architectural concrete
        03470 - Tilt-up precast concrete
        03480 - Precast concrete specialties

2.   Formwork and reinforcement shall not be measured separately but shall be described with the item.

3.   Slabs, walls, covers etc. shall be measured in square feet. Beams, sills, copings, etc. shall be measured in feet. Individual items shall be enumerated.

4.   Structural precast post-tensioned concrete shall be measured in the same manner as post-tensioned cast-in-place concrete, as described in 03300 – Cast-in-Place Concrete, item 6 above.

03500 - CEMENTITIOUS DECKS AND UNDERLAYMENT

1.   Cementitious decks and underlayment shall be measured in the following categories:

        03510 - Cementitious roof deck
        03520 - Lightweight concrete roof insulation
        03530 - Concrete topping
        03540 - Cementitious underlayment

2.   All work in this category shall be measured in square yards.

03600 - GROUTS

1. Grouting shall be measured in feet, or may be enumerated, as appropriate.

03900 - CONCRETE RESTORATION AND CLEANING

1. Concrete restoration and cleaning shall be measured in the following categories:

    03910 - Concrete cleaning
    03920 - Concrete resurfacing
    03930 - Concrete rehabilitation

2. Work in this category shall normally be measured in square yards.

GENERALLY

1.　The section "General Rules" is to be read in conjunction with this Division.

2.　The major items of masonry work shall be measured in square feet. No deductions shall be made for openings not exceeding 10 square feet.

3.　The measurement of masonry shall be deemed to include normal cleaning, building in or cutting chases for pipes, ducts and conduits, for cutting around, against and to the underside of concrete or steel members, and building in anchor bolts, sleeves, brackets and similar items. Special sized units to allow bonding with other materials shall also be deemed included.

4.　Masonry shall be measured under the following headings:

　　1.　Facings
　　2.　Backings to facings
　　3.　Walls and partitions
　　4.　Furring to walls
　　5.　Fire protection to structural steelwork
　　6.　Chimney stacks
　　7.　Damp courses

5.　Sections (04060) - Mortar materials and (04070) – Grout, used in the installation of masonry shall be included in the measurement of the masonry item.

04080 - MASONRY ANCHORAGE AND REINFORCEMENT

1.　Joint reinforcement shall be measured in feet.

2.　Ties, shoe tile units, anchors and the like shall be enumerated.

3.　Reinforcing steel shall be measured in pounds or feet.

4.　Setting only steel lintels shall be measured in pounds and the number shall be stated.

04090 - MASONRY ACCESSORIES

1.　Control and expansion joints shall be measured in feet.

2.　Embedded flashings integral with masonry shall be measured in feet.

04200 - MASONRY UNITS

1. Unit masonry shall be measured in the following categories:

    04210 - Clay masonry units
    04220 - Concrete masonry units
    04230 - Reinforced unit masonry
    04270 - Glass masonry units

2. Reinforced block and tile lintels shall be measured in feet.

3. Masonry units in special shapes shall be enumerated.

4. The formation of decorative patterns and features shall be measured in square feet as "extra labour and material", describing the decorative pattern or feature.

5. Special units of differing thickness from the main unit, where required at sills, heads and the like, shall be measured in feet.

6. Chimney caps shall be enumerated.

7. Silicone treatment to the surface of masonry shall be measured in square feet.

04400 - STONE

1. Stone shall be measured in the following categories:

    04410 - Natural and cut stone
    04420 - Collected stone
    04430 - Quarried stone

2. Copings, sills, jambs, mullions and the like shall be measured in feet.

3. Keystones, isolated lettered stones, and similar individual items shall be enumerated.

04500 - REFRACTORIES

1. Refractories shall be measured in the following categories:

    04550 - Flue liners
    04560 - Combustion chambers
    04580 - Refractory brick

2. Flue liners shall be measured in feet. Combustion chambers shall be measured in square feet, with the floor, walls and roof kept separate. Alternatively, combustion chambers may be enumerated. Refractory brick shall be measured in square feet.

04600 - CORROSION RESISTANT MASONRY

1. Corrosion resistant masonry shall be measured in the following categories:

    04610 - Chemical resistant brick
    04620 - Vitrified clay liner plates

2. Chemical resistant brick and vitrified clay liner plates shall be measured in accordance with the Method of Measurement for Masonry Units.

04700 - SIMULATED MASONRY

1. Mineral, epoxy, fibreglass and other types of simulated masonry shall be measured in accordance with the Method of Measurement for Masonry Units.

04900 - MASONRY RESTORATION AND CLEANING

1. Masonry restoration, alterations and cleaning shall be measured in the following categories:

    04910 - Unit masonry restoration
    04920 - Stone restoration
    04930 - Unit masonry cleaning
    04940 - Stone cleaning

2. The type of masonry shall be described. Interior and exterior work shall be measured separately.

3. Cutting openings shall be enumerated.

4. Making good jambs to new openings shall be measured in feet.

04900 - MASONRY RESTORATION AND CLEANING (Continued)

5.   Cutting, toothing and bonding new work to existing shall be measured in feet.

6.   Blocking up existing openings shall be enumerated.

7.   Masonry work in raising old walls shall be kept separate, and the height above ground stated. Preparation of existing walls for raising shall be measured in feet.

8.   Shoring and needling, or propping for insertion of new lintels shall be enumerated, stating the size of the opening, and thickness of the wall.

GENERALLY

1.   The section "General Rules" is to be read in conjunction with this Division.

2.   Unless otherwise stated, structural steel shall be measured by mass in tons or pounds. The weight of structural sections shall be calculated from the theoretical mass of the section as detailed by the Canadian Institute of Steel Construction.

05100 - STRUCTURAL METAL FRAMING

1.   Structural metal framing shall be measured in the following categories:

     05120 - Structural steel
     05140 - Structural aluminum
     05150 - Wire rope assemblies
     05160 - Metal framing systems

2.   Within these categories, as appropriate, each differing structural section shall be given separately and described in accordance with its function, e.g. column, beam, member of roof truss, etc. Members of a built-up section shall be grouped under a suitable heading.

3.   Metal fastenings for joining metals together shall be given by mass, and grouped as rivets, welds, or bolts, nuts and washers.

4.   The overall length, depth, span and load capacity of open web joists shall be given.

05200 - METAL JOISTS

1.   Non-framed metal joists shall be measured in the following categories:

     05210 - Steel joists
     05250 - Aluminum joists
     05260 - Composite joist assemblies

2.   Related bridging, anchors and accessories shall be included with these categories.

05300 - METAL DECK

1. Metal deck shall be measured in the following categories:

    05310 - Steel deck
    05320 - Raceway deck systems
    05330 - Aluminum deck
    05340 - Acoustical metal deck

2. Metal decking shall be measured in square feet. Raking and circular cutting shall each be measured in feet.

3. Gutters, eavestroughs, end fillers and other special shapes shall be measured in feet. Ends, mitres, junctions etc., shall be enumerated.

4. Holes, notches, pipe flashings, etc. shall be enumerated.

05400 - COLD-FORMED METAL FRAMING

1. Cold-formed metal framing shall be measured in the following categories:

    05410 - Load-bearing metal studs
    05420 - Cold-formed metal joists
    05450 - Metal supports

2. Load-bearing metal stud walls and partitions shall be measured in square feet.

3. Cold-formed metal joists shall be measured in feet.

4. Metal supports shall be enumerated.

05500 - METAL FABRICATIONS

1. Metal fabrications shall be measured in the following categories:

    05510 - Metal stairs and ladders
    05520 - Handrails and railings
    05530 - Gratings
    05540 - Floor plates
    05550 - Stair treads and nosings
    05560 - Castings

05500 - METAL FABRICATIONS (Continued)

2.   The components of metal stairs shall be grouped under a brief description of the stairs; the description shall include the method of fabrication.   The individual components shall be measured in feet, or enumerated, as appropriate.

3.   Ladders shall be enumerated.

4.   Handrails and railings shall be measured in feet.   Handrail brackets shall be enumerated.

5.   Gratings, floor plates, stair treads and nosings shall be measured in feet.

6.   Castings shall be measured in feet, or enumerated, as appropriate.

05700 - ORNAMENTAL METAL

1.   Ornamental metal shall be measured in the following categories:

> 05710 - Ornamental stairs
> 05715 - Prefabricated spiral stairs
> 05720 - Ornamental handrails and railings
> 05725 - Ornamental metal castings
> 05730 - Ornamental sheet metal

2.   Items in the above categories shall be measured in accordance with the principles set out in Section 05500 - Metal fabrications.

05800 - EXPANSION CONTROL

1.   Expansion control shall be measured in the following categories:

> 05810 - Expansion joint cover assemblies
> 05820 - Slide bearings
> 05830 - Bridge expansion joint assemblies

2.   Items in the above categories shall be measured in feet, or enumerated, as appropriate.

GENERALLY

1.   The section "General Rules" is to be read in conjunction with this Division.

2.   Lumber and finishing trim shall be measured in feet unless otherwise stated. Building paper and felt, wood, plywood and board sheathing, soffits and panelling shall be measured in square feet. Small blockings, backboards and the like shall be enumerated.   Rough hardware fixings, other than nails and screws, shall be enumerated; drilling through wood and other materials in this Division shall be deemed included in the fixing item.

3.   The dimensions of lumber shall be given as finished metric sizes,

4.   Lumber specified to be in lengths exceeding 20 feet shall be kept separate and given in 2 feet stages.

5.   Fasteners shall be enumerated within each category.

6.   The treatment of wood products to increase their durability, retard burning and prevent attack by insects shall be described with the item, or group of items, to which the treatment applies.

06100 - ROUGH CARPENTRY

1.   Rough carpentry shall be measured in the following categories:

       06110 - Wood framing
       06120 - Structural panels
       06130 - Heavy timber construction
       06140 - Treated wood foundations
       06150 - Wood decking
       06160 - Sheathing
       06170 - Prefabricated structural wood
       06180 - Glued-laminated construction

06100 - ROUGH CARPENTRY (Continued)

2. Additional information shall be given in the description of particular items within the above categories as follows:

1. 06110 - Wood framing

    1. Stud walls exceeding 10 feet in height shall be so described, and shall be kept separate in 2 feet increments

    2. Bridging shall be measured over the joists and the depth and centres of the joists shall be stated.

2. 06130 - Heavy timber construction

    1. The individual components of timber trusses shall be kept separate.

3. 06150 - Wood decking

    1. Work in this category is normally material which remains exposed.

4. 06160 - Sheathing

    1. Work to sloping or pitched surfaces exceeding 10° shall be kept separate, stating the pitch

    2. Diagonal work shall be kept separate

    3. Gypsum sheathing over or under wood framing, when used as an unfinished fire stop, is included in this category.

5. 06170 - Prefabricated structural wood

    1. Wood chord metal joists shall be measured in feet.

    2. Prefabricated wood trusses shall be enumerated.

06200 - FINISH CARPENTRY

1. Finish carpentry shall be measured in the following categories:

    06220 - Millwork
    06250 - Prefinished paneling
    06260 - Board paneling
    06270 - Closet and utility wood shelving

2. The above categories include the fabrication and installation of site built and site finished cabinets, moulding and trim and the installation of cabinet hardware.

3. Shelving exceeding 1 foot wide, and slatted shelving, shall be measured in square feet.

4. Wood, composition, plywood and plastic siding may be measured in the above categories instead of in Division 7.

06400 - ARCHITECTURAL WOODWORK

1. Architectural woodwork shall be measured in the following categories:

    06410 - Custom cabinets
    06415 - Countertops
    06420 - Paneling
    06430 - Wood stairs and railings
    06450 - Standing and running trim
    06460 - Wood frames
    06470 - Screens, blinds and shutters

2. The above categories include the shop fabrication and prefinishing of woodwork requiring expert craftsmanship and joinery, and the installation of fasteners and hardware.

3. Custom casework, comprising plastic laminate faced, shop finished or unfinished wood cabinets shall be enumerated.

4. Stairwork comprising treads, risers, nosings, balusters and newel posts shall be enumerated.

06500 - STRUCTURAL PLASTICS

1. Structural plastic framing elements, and other plastic fabrications, including erection and anchorage, shall be measured in this category.

2. The method of measurement shall be the same as for the comparable items described previously in this Division.

06600 - PLASTIC FABRICATIONS

1. Construction units and assemblies using plastic material shall be measured in this category.

2. The method of measurement shall be the same as for the comparable items described previously in this Division.

06900 - WOOD AND PLASTIC RESTORATION AND CLEANING

1. Wood and plastic restoration and cleaning shall be measured in the following categories:

    06910 - Wood restoration and cleaning
    06920 - Plastic restoration and cleaning

2. Work in this category may be measured in feet, square feet, or enumerated as appropriate.

GENERALLY

1. The section "General Rules" is to be read in conjunction with this Division.

2. Unless otherwise stated, all items in this Division shall be measured in square feet.

3. Vertical, horizontal, sloped, curved surfaces and areas inside tanks shall be measured separately.

4. In respect to roofing, the nature of the surface to receive the roofing, and the height above grade at which the work will be executed, shall be given.

5. Special testing procedures, where required, shall be given, stating the number of tests to be undertaken, the method of test execution and subsequent repair.

07100 - DAMPPROOFING AND WATERPROOFING

1. Dampproofing refers to materials which are not subject to hydrostatic pressure, while waterproofing refers to materials which are subject to continuous or intermittent hydrostatic pressure. Dampproofing and waterproofing shall be measured in the following categories:

   07110 - Dampproofing
   07120 - Built-up bituminous waterproofing
   07130 - Sheet waterproofing
   07140 - Fluid-applied waterproofing
   07150 - Sheet metal waterproofing
   07170 - Bentonite waterproofing
   07180 - Traffic coatings
   07190 - Water repellents

2. Protection covering shall be measured separately.

3. Deductions shall be made for openings exceeding 40 square feet.

4. Work to reglets, chases and similar items shall be measured in feet.

5. Work around, or openings for, pipes, sleeves, drains, bolts or other similar items shall be enumerated.

6. The material to which water repellent is to be applied shall be stated.

07200 - THERMAL PROTECTION

1.   Thermal protection shall be measured under the following categories:

   07210 - Building insulation
   07220 - Roof and deck insulation
   07240 - Exterior insulation and finish systems (EIFS)
   07260 - Vapour retarders
   07270 - Air barriers

2.   Deductions shall be made for openings exceeding 40 square feet.

3.   The location to which the thermal insulation is to be applied shall be stated.

4.   Insulation placed inside formwork shall be so stated.

5.   Insulation placed by blowing shall be so stated.

6.   Sprayed insulation exceeding 12 inches high shall be measured separately.

7.   Composite exterior insulation and finish systems shall be measured as one item, and described as site or shop applied.

07300 - SHINGLES, ROOF TILES AND ROOF COVERINGS

1.   Shingles, roof tiles and roof coverings shall be measured in the following categories:

   07310 - Shingles
   07320 - Roof tiles
   07330 - Roof coverings

2.   Deduction shall be made for openings exceeding 10 square feet.

3.   The component parts of shingle roofing, i.e. preparatory work, sheathing paper, underlayment and surfacing shall be given.

4.   The component parts of tile roofing i.e. preparatory work, sheathing paper, underlayment, fixing media and surfacing shall be given.

07400 - ROOFING AND SIDING PANELS

1. Manufactured roofing and siding shall be measured in the following categories:

    07410 - Manufactured roof and wall panels
    07420 - Plastic roof and wall panels
    07430 - Composite panels
    07440 - Faced panels
    07450 - Fibre-reinforced cementitious panels
    07460 - Siding
    07470 - Wood roof and wall panels
    07480 - Exterior wall assemblies

2. Wood, plywood, composition and plastic sidings may be measured in Division 6, category 06200.

07500 - MEMBRANE ROOFING

1. Membrane roofing shall be measured in the following categories:

    07510 - Built-up bituminous roofing
    07520 - Cold-applied bituminous roofing
    07530 - Elastomeric membrane roofing
    07540 - Thermoplastic membrane roofing
    07550 - Modified bituminous membrane roofing
    07560 - Fluid-applied roofing
    07570 - Coated foamed roofing
    07580 - Roll roofing
    07590 - Roof maintenance and repairs

2. The component parts of membrane roofing i.e. preparatory work, sheathing paper, primer, vapour barrier, underlayment, insulation, felt, asphalt, membrane, surfacing, gravel, as applicable to the particular material, shall be given.

07600 - FLASHING AND SHEET METAL

1. Flashing and sheet metal shall be measured in the following categories:

    07610 - Sheet metal roofing
    07620 - Sheet metal flashing and trim
    07630 - Sheet metal roofing specialties
    07650 - Flexible flashing

2. The component parts of sheet metal roofing, i.e. preparatory work, sheathing paper, primer, underlayment, surfacing shall be given.

3. Standing seams, welts and drips forming part of the general roof area shall be given in the item of roofing.

4. Flashing, gutters, valleys, hips, starter and underlayment strips, cants, etc., shall be separately measured in feet.

07700 - ROOF SPECIALITIES AND ACCESSORIES

1. Roof specialties and accessories shall be measured in the following categories:

    07710 - Manufactured roof specialties
    07720 - Roof accessories
    07730 - Roof pavers

2. Copings, counterflashing systems, gravel stops, fascias, reglets and the like, shall be separately measured in feet.

3. Roof hatches, vents, scuppers and the like shall be separately enumerated.

4. Roof pavers shall be measured in square feet.

07800 - FIRE AND SMOKE PROTECTION

1. Fire and smoke protection shall be measured in the following categories:

    07810 - Applied fireproofing
    07820 - Board fireproofing
    07840 - Firestopping

2. Fire and smoke protection shall be measured in feet or in square feet as appropriate.

07900 - JOINT SEALERS

1. Joint sealers shall be measured in the following categories:

    07910 - Preformed joint seals
    07920 - Joint sealants

2. Joint fillers, gaskets and caulking shall be separately measured in feet. Where special equipment methods are required to be employed, this shall be given.

GENERALLY

1.   The section "General Rules" is to be read in conjunction with this Division.

2.   Unless otherwise stated all items in this Division shall be enumerated.

3.   Temporary supports, bracing and protection of components prior to building in shall be measured as a separate item.

4.   Final cleaning of units shall be measured as a separate item.

5.   Wood surfaces to receive a clear finish shall be so described.

6.   Any testing shall be measured as a separate item.

7.   Hardware items, unless part of a pre-packaged assembly, shall be measured in Section 08700 - Hardware.

8.   Glazing and glazing accessories may be included with the appropriate door, or may be measured in Section 08800 - Glazing.

9.   Wood frames, which are not provided as part of Section 08250 - Door Opening Assemblies, shall be measured in Division 6.

10. A description of blockings and stiffeners to accommodate finishing hardware shall be included in the description of doors.

11. Blanking out, reinforcing, drilling and tapping to receive standard and heavy duty mortise hinges, closers, keeps, etc. from templates received from the finishing hardware supplier, together with removable stops, mutes, plaster grounds and anchors shall be included in the description of frames.

08100 - METAL DOORS AND FRAMES

1.   Metal doors and frames shall be measured in the following categories:

> 08110 - Steel doors and frames
> 08120 - Aluminum doors and frames
> 08130 - Stainless steel doors and frames
> 08140 - Bronze doors and frames
> 08150 - Preassembled metal door and frame units
> 08160 - Sliding metal doors and grilles
> 08180 - Metal screen and storm doors

2   08100 - METAL DOORS AND FRAMES (Continued)

2. Louvres fabricated integrally with doors and frames shall be described with the appropriate door or frame. Louvres which are field inserted in doors and frames shall be measured for supply under Divisions 10 or 15, and shall be enumerated for fixing only in this Section.

3. Combination frames, incorporating side and transom lights, shall be measured in feet under their constituent parts, i.e. frame, transom, mullion, sill. Connections between each part shall be enumerated, by type.

4. The installation of doors, frames and combination frames shall each be enumerated separately.

08200 - WOOD AND PLASTIC DOORS

1. Wood and plastic doors shall be measured in the following categories:

    08210 - Wood doors
    08220 - Plastic doors
    08250 - Preassembled wood and plastic door and frame units
    08260 - Sliding wood and plastic doors
    08280 - Wood and plastic storm and screen doors

2. Wood louvres and factory installed metal louvres for fire rated doors shall be described with the appropriate door. Metal louvres which are field inserted in non-fire rated doors shall be measured for supply in Divisions 10 or 15, and shall be enumerated for fixing only in this Section.

3. The installation of doors shall be separately enumerated.

08300 - SPECIALTY DOORS

1. Specialty doors and assemblies, including hardware, controls, operators and drive mechanisms shall be measured in the following categories:

    08310 - Access doors and panels
    08320 - Detention doors and frames
    08330 - Coiling doors and grilles
    08340 - Special function doors
    08350 - Folding doors and grilles
    08360 - Overhead doors
    08370 - Vertical lift doors
    08380 - Traffic doors
    08390 - Pressure-resistant doors

2. The installation of special doors shall each be separately enumerated.

08400 - ENTRANCES AND STOREFRONTS

1. Entrances and storefronts are typically one storey systems. Each shall be measured separately, for supply and installation, in the following categories:

    08410 - Metal-framed storefronts
    08450 - All-glass entrances and storefronts
    08460 - Automatic entrance doors
    08470 - Revolving entrance doors
    08480 - Balanced entrance doors
    08490 - Sliding storefronts

2. Within each category, each section shall be preceded by a descriptive preamble which shall include a short description of the components, the overall dimensions of the unit and the material to which it will be fixed.

3. Glass and glazing shall be measured in accordance with Section 08800. Alternatively, where appropriate, glass and glazing may be included with the description of the entrance or storefront.

4. Entrance doors, screens, automatic door operators, metal anchors and the like shall be enumerated. Door thresholds shall be measured in feet and the number stated. Handrails shall be measured in feet. Special facings shall be measured in square feet and shall include the supporting framework. Structural steel reinforcing members shall be measured in pounds.

08400 - ENTRANCES AND STOREFRONTS (Continued)

5. Storefronts shall be measured in accordance with the methods of measurement in the preceding paragraph as far as they apply. Spandrel and infill panels shall be enumerated. Insulation applied in the field shall be measured in square feet. Window cleaning anchors, including reinforcement, shall be enumerated. Hoisting, if the responsibility of this contractor, shall be given as an item.

08500 - WINDOWS

1. Windows shall be measured in the following categories:

    08510 - Steel windows
    08520 - Aluminum windows
    08530 - Stainless steel windows
    08540 - Bronze windows
    08550 - Wood windows
    08560 - Plastic windows
    08570 - Composite windows
    08580 - Special function windows

2. Fixed and operable windows used singly, or in multiples, shall be enumerated separately. The method of operation of operable windows, (sliding, hung, etc.), shall be given in the description.

3. Window units with louvre blinds set integrally between glass panels shall be so described.

4. Jalousies shall be enumerated.

5. Components such as main frame, mullion, transom, sill shall be measured separately, in feet. Connections between components shall be enumerated, by type.

6. Where windows are factory glazed, the glazing beads, glass and glazing, and solar plastic film if required, shall be included with the window. Otherwise, glazing beads shall be described with the window, and glass and glazing shall be measured in Section 08800.

7. The installation of windows shall be enumerated, stating overall size, and whether installed from the outside or inside.

08600 - SKYLIGHTS

1.   Skylights shall be measured in the following categories:

    08610 - Roof windows
    08620 - Unit skylights
    08630 - Metal-framed skylights

08700 - HARDWARE

1.   Hardware shall be measured in the following categories:

    08710 - Door hardware
    08720 - Weatherstripping and seals
    08740 - Electro-mechanical hardware
    08750 - Window hardware
    08770 - Door and window accessories
    08790 - Special function hardware

2.   Hardware and gasketing for doors and windows not specifically supplied as part of the manufactured item shall be measured in this Section. (Note: Hardware required for items supplied in Divisions 6, 10 and 12 shall be included with those Divisions.)

3.   The installation of hardware shall normally be measured separately from its supply.

4.   Matching screws shall be deemed to be included in the supply of hardware.

5.   Preparing wood, metal, etc., to receive hardware (e.g. sinking, boring, grooving, mortising,) shall be deemed to be included with the appropriate installation item.

6.   Butts and hinges shall be measured in pairs.

7.   Weatherstripping shall be measured in feet.

8.   Keying of locks shall be given as a separate item stating number of keys per item, master keying and any requirement to match an existing system.

08800 - GLAZING

1. Glass and glazing shall be measured in the following categories:

   08810 - Glass
   08830 - Mirrors
   08840 - Plastic glazing
   08850 - Glazing accessories

2. All types of glass and glazing used for doors, windows, sidelights, transoms, entrances, storefronts, curtain walls, framed skylights and balustrades not specifically supplied as part of the manufactured item shall be measured in this Section.

3. Glass and plastic glazing shall be measured in square feet. Each light shall be measured to the next increment of 1 inch in each direction for either single glass or sealed units.

4. Lights of glass of irregular shape shall be measured to the nearest rectangular area, in accordance with the previous paragraph, and described as "in irregular areas." Circular cutting shall be measured in feet.

5. Lights of glass which are bent shall be enumerated, and the radius of the bend stated.

6. Interior and exterior glass and glazing shall be given separately. If scaffolding or special hoisting is required, this shall be stated.

7. Setting blocks, shims, splines, clips and other accessories shall be deemed to be included in the description of glass and glazing.

8. Glazing compound, tape, and the removal and refixing of glazing beads shall be measured in feet.

9. Edge work shall be measured in feet.

10. Holes drilled or cut in glass shall be enumerated, giving details of the hole and the glass.

11. Grinding, sandblasting, acid etching, embossing, etc., shall be enumerated.

12. The length of guarantee for sealed units shall be stated.

08800 – GLAZING (Continued)

13.   Stained glass work and solar plastic film shall be measured in Division 12.

14.   Glazing integral with casework, food service equipment, telephone enclosures and detention equipment is measured with the item in the appropriate Division.

08900 - GLAZED CURTAIN WALL

1.   Glazed curtain walls are typically designed for multistorey construction but may be applied to single storey structures.   They shall be measured for supply and installation in the following categories:

   08910 - Metal framed curtain walls
   08950 - Translucent wall and roof assemblies
   08960 - Sloped glazing assemblies
   08970 - Structural glass curtain walls

2.   Within each category, each section shall be preceded by a descriptive preamble which shall include a short description of the components, the overall dimensions of the unit and the material to which it will be fixed.

3.   Glass and glazing shall be measured in accordance with Section 08800. Alternatively, where appropriate, glass and glazing may be included with the description of the curtain wall.

4.   The principles of measurement previously described in Section 08100 - Metal doors and frames, and 08500 - Windows shall apply equally to this Section.

5.   Spandrel and infill panels shall be enumerated.

6.   Insulation applied in the field shall be measured in square feet.   Hoisting, if the responsibility of this contractor, shall be given as an item.

GENERALLY

1. The section "General Rules" is to be read in conjunction with this Division.

2. Finishes shall be measured in square feet.

3. Work exceeding 12 feet high shall be so described, and the height above the floor level given in 6 feet stages.

4. Where not otherwise apparent, work in this Division shall be stated to be either to floors, walls or ceilings.

5. Where work to landings is required to be stated, it refers to landings not exceeding 40 square feet. Landings exceeding 40 square feet shall be considered to be floors.

6. Exterior work shall be so stated.

09100 - METAL SUPPORT ASSEMBLIES

1. Metal support assemblies shall be measured in the following categories:

    09110 - Non-load-bearing wall framing
    09120 - Ceiling suspension
    09130 - Acoustical suspension

2. Deductions shall be made for openings exceeding 20 square feet.

09200 - PLASTER AND GYPSUM BOARD

1. Plaster and gypsum board shall be measured in the following categories:

    09205 - Furring and lathing
    09210 - Gypsum plaster
    09220 - Portland cement plaster
    09230 - Plaster fabrications
    09250 - Gypsum board
    09260 - Gypsum board assemblies

2. Deductions shall be made for openings exceeding 20 square feet.

3. Plaster and gypsum board to columns, isolated columns, beams, bulkheads, ducts and the like shall be so stated. Where the girth of such work does not exceed 6 feet, it shall be stated as not exceeding 3 feet girth, or exceeding 3 feet but not exceeding 6 feet girth.

09200 - PLASTER AND GYPSUM BOARD (Continued)

4. Gypsum board not exceeding 1 foot wide, unless caused by voids, shall be so stated.

5. Framings within plaster and gypsum board for recessed openings shall be enumerated.

6. Corner beads, casing beads, joint and strip reinforcement shall be measured in feet.

7. Angle beads, stops, casings, expansion joints, base screeds, wall mouldings and metal extrusions shall be measured in feet.

8. Plaster work to columns, isolated columns and beams shall be so stated.

9. No deductions shall be made for bases, mouldings, grounds, etc.

10. Cornices, mouldings, bases, friezes, etc. shall be measured their extreme length, in feet.

11. Column bases, caps and other enrichments shall be enumerated.

12. Patching in repair work, where partitions, bases, rails, etc. have been removed, shall be measured in feet.

13. Holes, notches, etc. in gypsum board shall be deemed included.

09300 - TILE

1. Tile shall be measured in the following categories:

    09310 - Ceramic tile
    09330 - Quarry tile
    09340 - Paver tile
    09350 - Glass mosaics
    09360 - Plastic tile
    09370 - Metal tile
    09380 - Cut natural stone tile

2. Deductions shall be made for openings exceeding 5 feet.

3. Tiles to floor and walls of swimming and therapeutic pools shall be so described.

09300 – TILE (Continued)

4. Tiles with rounded edges, internal and external angle tiles, coved base tiles, etc. shall be measured in feet.

5. Tiles rounded on two edges shall be enumerated.

6. Built up bases, jambs, treads, risers, scum gutters, etc., shall be measured in feet; special shaped tiles shall be included in the description.

7. Tiles forming letters and numerals shall be enumerated.

8. Tiling to pump bases, and other similar small items, shall be enumerated.

9. Ceramic tile towel bar holders, toilet paper roll holders, soap dishes and other ceramic tile toilet accessories shall be enumerated, and included in this Division.

09400 - TERRAZZO

1. Terrazzo shall be measured in the following categories:

    09410 - Portland cement terrazzo
    09420 - Precast terrazzo
    09430 - Conductive terrazzo
    09440 - Plastic matrix terrazzo

2. Deductions shall be made for openings exceeding 10 square feet.

3. Patterned work shall be so stated.

4. Accessories, such as division strips and finish sealers, shall be given in the description. The sizes of panels shall be stated.

5. Curbs and base shall be measured in feet. Base and border shall be measured as one item, in feet.

6. Work to stairs and landings shall be kept separate. Treads and risers shall be measured as one item, in feet, and the number of treads stated. Non-slip nosings, strings and aprons shall each be separately measured in feet.

7. Rebates to receive frames, gratings, and the like shall be measured in feet. Rebates and sinkings for mat frames shall be enumerated.

09400 - TERRAZZO (Continued)

8.   Features formed in precast work shall be measured in feet, or enumerated, as appropriate. Holes, notches and the like in precast work shall be enumerated.

9.   Small items, in both cast-in-place and precast items, shall be enumerated.

09500 - CEILINGS

1.   Ceiling shall be measured in the following categories:

> 09510 - Acoustical ceilings
> 09545 - Specialty ceilings
> 09550 - Mirror panel ceilings
> 09560 - Textured ceilings
> 09570 - Linear wood ceilings
> 09580 - Suspended decorative grids

2.   Deductions shall be made for openings exceeding 5 square feet.

3.   Surfaces not exceeding 1 foot wide, unless caused by voids, shall be measured in feet. Special borders shall be measured in feet.

4.   Ceilings to sides and soffits of beams shall be so described. Special corner joints shall be given in feet.

09600 - FLOORING

1.   Flooring shall be measured in the following categories:

> 09610 - Floor treatment
> 09620 - Specialty flooring
> 09630 - Masonry flooring
> 09650 - Resilient flooring
> 09660 - Static control flooring
> 09670 - Fluid-applied flooring
> 09680 - Carpet

2.   Deductions shall be made for openings exceeding 5 square feet in categories 09610, 09620 and 09630, and exceeding 10 square feet in all other categories.

3.   Work not exceeding 1 foot wide, unless caused by voids, shall be measured in feet.

09600 - FLOORING (Continued)

4.   Base, treads, nosings, risers, feature strips and the like shall be so described and measured in feet.

5.   Flooring to decorative patterns, borders, games courts, etc., shall be so described.

6.   Carpet to landings shall be so described.

7.   Carpet fixing at perimeters shall be measured in feet. Cutting and fitting carpet around obstructions shall be enumerated.

8.   Cover and threshold strips shall be measured in feet.

09700 - WALL FINISHES

1.   Wall finishes shall be measured in the following categories:

        09710 - Acoustical wall finishes
        09720 - Wall covering
        09730 - Wall carpet
        09740 - Flexible wood sheets
        09750 - Stone facing
        09770 - Special wall surfaces

2.   Deductions shall be made for openings exceeding 10 square feet.

3.   Wall finishes not exceeding 1 foot wide, unless caused by voids, shall be measured in feet.

4.   Border strips shall be measured in feet.

09800 - ACOUSTICAL TREATMENT

1.   Acoustical treatment shall be measured in the following categories:

        09810 - Acoustical space units
        09820 - Acoustical insulation and sealants
        09830 - Acoustical barriers
        09840 - Acoustical wall treatment

2.   Deductions shall be made for openings exceeding 10 square feet.

09800 - ACOUSTICAL TREATMENT (Continued)

3.   Surfaces not exceeding 1 foot wide, unless caused by voids, shall be measured in feet. Borders shall be measured in feet.

4.   Acoustical tile to sides and soffits of beams shall be measured in feet; the type of corner joint shall be stated.

5.   Holes, notches and the like shall be deemed included.

09900 - PAINTS AND COATINGS

1.   Paints and coatings shall be measured in the following categories:

    09910 - Exterior and interior painting
    09930 - Stains and transparent finishes
    09940 - Decorative finishes
    09960 - High-performance coatings
    09970 - Coatings for steel
    09980 - Coatings for concrete and masonry

2.   Deductions shall be made for openings exceeding 10 square feet.

3.   Work in confined areas shall be so described.

4.   Special decorative work, such as striped colours and dragged or patterned work, shall be so described.

5.   The contact area of the surface to be painted shall be measured. Allowances shall be made for corrugations, tongued and grooved surfaces, etc.

6.   Painting to surfaces not exceeding 1 foot wide, unless caused by voids, shall be measured in feet.

7.   Cut lines between changes of colour shall be measured in feet.

8.   Windows and doors shall be measured overall, both sides; no deduction shall be made for the area of glass.

09900 - PAINTS AND COATINGS (Continued)

9.　Balustrades, fencing and similar items shall be measured overall, both sides, between top and bottom rails. The extra area of posts above and below the rails shall be deemed included.

10.　Handrails and similar items shall be measured in feet; brackets shall be deemed included.

11.　Open web steel joists and steel lattice work shall be measured as a solid surface, both sides, based on the length and depth of the joist or lattice work.

12.　Games lines, parking lines and the like shall be measured in feet.

13.　Small tanks, pumps, motors and other equipment, valves and similar items shall be enumerated.

14.　Letters and numerals shall be enumerated.

15.　Test panels or mock-ups shall be enumerated.

16.　Testing shall be given as an item.

17.　Clean-up on completion shall be given as an item.

GENERALLY

1. The section "General Rules" is to be read in conjunction with this Division.

2. Unless otherwise stated, all items in this Division shall be enumerated.

10100 - VISUAL DISPLAY BOARDS

1. Visual display boards shall be measured in the following categories:

    10110 - Chalkboards
    10115 - Markerboards
    10120 - Tackboard and visual aid boards
    10130 - Operable board units
    10140 - Display track assemblies
    10145 - Visual aid board units

2. The description of the item shall include the method of fixing, and, where applicable, whether manually, mechanically or electrically operated.

10150 - COMPARTMENTS AND CUBICLES

1. Compartments and cubicles shall be measured in the following categories:

    10160 - Metal toilet compartments
    10165 - Plastic laminate toilet compartments
    10170 - Plastic toilet compartments
    10175 - Particleboard toilet compartments
    10180 - Stone toilet compartments
    10185 - Shower and dressing compartments
    10190 - Cubicles

2. Cubicle curtains and cubicle track and hardware shall be measured in Category 10190. Cubicle track may be measured in lineal feet, with bends, etc. enumerated.

3. The description of the compartment or cubicle shall state whether the item is wall hung, ceiling hung or floor mounted.

4. Toilet and bath accessories, which are to be provided by the manufacturer of the compartment or cubicle, shall be included in the description.

10200 - LOUVRES AND VENTS

1. Louvres and vents, which are not an integral part of the mechanical system, shall be measured in the following categories:

    10210 - Wall louvres
    10220 - Louvered equipment enclosures
    10225 - Door louvres
    10230 - Vents

10240 - GRILLES AND SCREENS

1. Exterior and interior screens, used for a variety of functions not limited to ventilation purposes, shall be measured in this category.

10260 - WALL AND CORNER GUARDS

1. Protective devices such as corner guards and bumper guards, unless of fabricated steel sections and plate, shall be measured in this category.

2. Continuous bumper guards shall be measured in feet; bends etc., shall be enumerated.

10270 - ACCESS FLOORING

1. Free standing access flooring including the floor finish, designed to form an underfloor cavity for mechanical or electrical distribution systems, shall be measured in this category.

2. Access flooring shall be measured in square feet.

10300 - FIREPLACES AND STOVES

1. Fireplaces and stoves shall be measured in the following categories:

    10305 - Manufactured fireplaces
    10310 - Fireplace specialties and accessories
    10320 - Stoves

2. Manufactured fireplace chimneys shall be measured in Category 10305, in lineal feet; bends, caps, etc., shall be enumerated.

3. Fireplace dampers, screens, doors, inserts, etc. shall be measured in Category 10310.

10340 - MANUFACTURED EXTERIOR SPECIALTIES

1.   Clocks, cupolas, spires, steeples, weathervanes and the like shall be measured in this category.

10350 - FLAGPOLES

1.   Automatic, ground-set and wall-mounted flagpoles shall be measured in this category, and shall include flags.

10400 - IDENTIFICATION DEVICES

1.   Identification devices shall be measured in the following categories:

> 10410 - Directories
> 10420 - Plaques
> 10430 - Exterior signage
> 10440 - Interior signage

10450 - PEDESTRIAN CONTROL DEVICES

1.   Detection and counting devices, portable posts and railings, rotary gates and turnstiles shall be measured in this category.

10500 - LOCKERS

1.   Lockers shall be measured in this category.

10530 - PROTECTIVE COVERS

1.   Awnings, canopies, car shelters, walkway coverings and the like shall be measured in this category.

10550 - POSTAL SPECIALTIES

1.   Postal specialties shall be measured in this category.

10600 - PARTITIONS

1. Partitions shall be measured in the following categories:

    10605 - Wire mesh partitions
    10610 - Folding gates
    10615 - Demountable partitions
    10630 - Portable partitions, screens and panels
    10650 - Operable partitions

2. Wire mesh partitions shall be measured in feet stating the height.

3. Demountable partitions shall be measured in feet stating the height. Doors supplied by the partition manufacturer shall be measured as extra over the cost of the partition.

10670 - STORAGE SHELVING

1. Storage shelving shall be measured in this category.

2. Open, manufactured shelving for general storage, as opposed to specific items, shall be measured in this category.

10700 - EXTERIOR PROTECTION

1. Exterior protection shall be measured in the following categories:

    10705 - Exterior sun control devices
    10710 - Exterior shutters
    10715 - Storm panels
    10720 - Exterior louvres

10800 - TOILET AND BATH ACCESSORIES

1. Toilet and bath accessories shall be measured in the following categories:

    10810 - Toilet accessories
    10820 - Bath accessories
    10830 - Laundry accessories

10900 - WARDROBE AND CLOSET SPECIALTIES

1. Manufactured hat and coat racks, and other specialties for storage of clothing, shall be measured in this category.

GENERALLY

1.   The section "General Rules" is to be read in conjunction with this Division.

2.   All items in this Division, unless otherwise stated, shall be enumerated.

3.   Many items in this Division are of a highly specialized nature, beyond the scope of normal building construction. A recommended method of measurement for such items has not been included herein.

11010 - MAINTENANCE EQUIPMENT

1.   Floor and wall cleaning equipment, vacuum cleaning systems and window washing systems shall be measured in this category.

2.   Within this category, guide and other rails shall be measured in feet.

11020 - SECURITY AND VAULT EQUIPMENT

1.   Security and vault equipment shall be measured in this category.

11040 - ECCLESIASTICAL EQUIPMENT

1.   Ecclesiastical equipment shall be measured in this category.

2.   Chancel rails shall be measured in feet.

11050 - LIBRARY EQUIPMENT

1.   Library equipment shall be measured in this category.

2.   Shelving shall be measured in feet.

11060 - THEATRE AND STAGE EQUIPMENT

1.   Acoustical shells, folding and portable stages and stage curtains shall be measured in this category.

11160 - LOADING DOCK EQUIPMENT

1.   Loading dock equipment shall be measured in this category.

11170 - SOLID WASTE HANDLING EQUIPMENT

1. Garbage chutes shall be measured in this category.

2. Chutes shall be measured in feet. Access doors, control doors, collectors and the like shall be enumerated.

11400 - FOOD SERVICE EQUIPMENT

1. Food service equipment shall be measured in the following categories:

    11405 - Food storage equipment
    11410 - Food preparation equipment
    11420 - Food cooking equipment
    11425 - Hood and ventilation equipment
    11430 - Food dispensing equipment
    11435 - Ice machines
    11440 - Cleaning and disposal equipment

2. Within the above categories, continuous counter tops may be measured in feet or enumerated.

11450 - RESIDENTIAL EQUIPMENT

1. Residential appliances, residential kitchen equipment, retractable stairs and the like shall be measured in this category.

11600 - LABORATORY EQUIPMENT

1. Laboratory equipment shall be measured in this category. Continuous counter tops may be measured in feet or enumerated.

GENERALLY

1. The section "General Rules" is to be read in conjunction with this Division.

2. Unless otherwise stated, all items in this Division shall be enumerated.

12100 - ARTWORK

1. Stained glass work shall be measured in this category.

12300 - MANUFACTURED CASEWORK

1. Manufactured casework shall be measured in the following categories:

    12310 - Manufactured metal casework
    12320 - Manufactured wood casework
    12350 - Specialty casework

2. The work in this Section applies to stock design cabinets and other casework units, manufactured from steel, wood and plastic laminate for a variety of uses. Site built, and site finished casework, shall be measured in Division 6.

12400 - FURNISHINGS AND ACCESSORIES

1. Furnishings and accessories shall be measured in the following categories:

    12440 - Bath furnishings
    12480 - Rugs and mats
    12490 - Window treatments

2. The description of blinds and shades shall include whether surface mounted, interior mounted or mounted between glass.

3. Solar control film shall be measured in square feet.

4. Track for hospital privacy curtains and the like shall be measured in feet.

5. Draperies and curtains shall be enumerated by panels, the description shall include the percentage of fullness required.

6. The description of stage, theatre or proscenium draperies shall include details of contour draping, control, traverse, rigging, counterweights, battens, tracks and all other required components.

12600 - MULTIPLE SEATING

1. Multiple seating shall be measured in the following categories:

> 12610 - Fixed audience seating
> 12630 - Stadium and arena seating
> 12660 - Telescoping stands
> 12670 - Pews and benches

12800 - INTERIOR PLANTS AND PLANTERS

1. Interior plants and planters shall be measured in the following categories:

> 12810 - Interior live plants
> 12830 - Interior planters
> 12840 - Interior landscape accessories

GENERALLY

1. The section "General Rules" is to be read in conjunction with this Division.

2. Many items in this Division are of a highly specialized nature, beyond the scope of normal building construction. A recommended method of measurement for such items has not been included herein.

13030 - SPECIAL PURPOSE ROOMS

1. Special purpose rooms, including cold storage rooms, saunas and vaults shall be measured in this category.

2. Items in these categories may be enumerated or measured in detail in accordance with the method of measurement for the appropriate Divisions.

13090 - RADIATION PROTECTION

1. Radiation shielding components and structures for protection against radio frequency, e-ray and nuclear radiation shall be measured in this category.

2. Sub-surface materials, such as concrete, masonry etc. shall be measured in their appropriate Division.

3. Sheet materials shall generally be measured in square feet. Deductions shall be made for openings exceeding 5 square feet. All additional materials, to give protection at joints, corners, openings, screw holes etc. shall be measured in feet, or enumerated, as appropriate. Surface application to doors, frames, hatches, duct and pipe openings shall be enumerated.

4. Window and door frames, doors, louvres, pass throughs and other items specially fabricated for radiation applications shall be enumerated.

13150 - SWIMMING POOLS

1. Swimming pools shall normally be measured in detail in accordance with the method of measurement for the appropriate Divisions.

13170 - TUBS AND POOLS

1. Tubs and pools, including hot tubs and therapeutic pools, shall be enumerated and measured in this category.

13185 - KENNELS AND ANIMAL SHELTERS

1. Kennels and animal shelters shall normally be measured in detail in accordance with the method of measurement for the appropriate Divisions. Small individual items may be enumerated and included in this category.

13200 - STORAGE TANKS

1. Storage tanks shall be measured in this category.

2. Items in this category may be measured in detail in accordance with the method of measurement for the appropriate Divisions or, if small in size, may be enumerated.

13900 - FIRE SUPPRESSION

1. Fire suppression shall be measured in the following categories:

    13920 - Fire pumps
    13930 - Wet-pipe suppression sprinklers
    13935 - Dry-pipe fire suppression sprinklers
    13950 - Deluge fire suppression systems
    13975 - Standpipes and hoses

2. Pipework shall be measured in feet; pumps, fittings, valves, hangers, supports, fire stopping, hoses etc. shall be enumerated.

GENERALLY

1. The section "General Rules" is to be read in conjunction with this Division.

2. Many items in this Division are of a highly specialized nature, beyond the scope of normal building construction. A recommended method of measurement for such items has not been included herein.

3. All items in this Division, unless otherwise stated, shall be enumerated.

14100 - DUMBWAITERS

1. Dumbwaiters shall be measured in the following categories:

    14110 - Manual dumbwaiters
    14120 - Electric dumbwaiters
    14140 - Hydraulic dumbwaiters

14200 - ELEVATORS

1. Elevators shall be measured in the following categories:

    14210 - Electric traction elevators
    14240 - Hydraulic elevators

2. Within the above categories, passenger, service and freight elevators shall each be kept separate.

14300 - ESCALATORS AND MOVING WALKS

1. Escalators and moving walks shall be measured in this category.

14400 - LIFTS

1. Lifts shall be measured in the following categories:

    14410 - People lifts
    14420 - Wheelchair lifts
    14430 - Platform lifts
    14440 - Sidewalk lifts
    14450 - Vehicle lifts

14500 - MATERIAL HANDLING

1. Laundry, linen and refuse chutes shall be measured in this category:

    14560 - Chutes

2. Chutes may be enumerated, or measured in detail. Where measured in detail, straight lengths shall be measured in feet and all other items shall be enumerated.

GENERALLY

1. The section "General Rules" is to be read in conjunction with this Division.

2. Work within this Division shall commence, or terminate, 3 feet from the outside face of the structure.

3. Pipework shall be measured in feet; fittings and valves shall be enumerated. No deduction in pipe lengths shall be made for fittings not exceeding 9 inches in diameter. Buried piping shall be so described.

4. With the exception of ductwork and mechanical insulation, all other items in this Division shall be enumerated. The method of measurement for ductwork and for mechanical insulation is detailed in the appropriate Section.

5. Items which are common to various Sections within this Division shall be measured separately with each Section. E.g. Hangers and supports, sleeves, fire stopping, roof flashings.

6. Vibration isolation materials shall be described with the item of equipment to which they relate.

CLASSIFICATIONS

1. The various classifications within the scope of "General Requirements" for this Division shall be measured and priced as "Items", unless a specific mode of measurement is recommended, in the following categories:

    1. Certificates and fees

        Include charges pertaining to fees, permits and licenses required for plumbing permit, Department of Labour, welding tests and other similar requirements.

    2. Liability and protection

        Include providing for errors, and protection of finishes.

    3. Record drawings

        Include the cost of producing as built drawings, when or where changes have been made from original drawings.

CLASSIFICATIONS (Continued)

1. 4. Shop drawings

   Include processing and checking shop drawings.

   5. Operating instructions and maintenance manuals

   Include providing written operating instructions and maintenance manuals. Where required, shall also include the use of labour, fuel, water and other materials.

   6. Contractor's shop

   Include:

   1. Providing, maintaining and removing all site offices, storage sheds, welfare accommodation and similar buildings, together with furniture, office equipment, services, and including all attendance thereon, heating and air conditioning if required.

   .2 Installing and all charges for telephone and facsimile facilities.

   7. Temporary and trial usage

   If part of the system is used on a temporary or trial basis before completion, include adjusting, oiling, greasing and other similar requirements upon final completion.

   8. Insurances

   Include all contract and labour insurance, including Public Liability, Unemployment, Workmen's Compensation, Hospital, Vacation, Calamity and Marine.

   9. Guarantee

   Include a guarantee to cover defects in materials and workmanship for a specified period of time.

   10. Preparation for painting

   Include cleaning surfaces ready for painting and identification by Division 9.

CLASSIFICATIONS (Continued)

1.   11.   Valve tags and charts

Include providing valve tags and charts.

12.   Wall plates and access doors

Include providing wall plates and access doors.

13.   Bases and supports

Include steel bases or stands for mechanical equipment unless specifically measured with the item concerned. Include all miscellaneous steelwork related to this Division including that required for seismic bracing.

14.   Temporary plumbing

Include all labour, material, permits and fees. Alternatively, it shall be measured in detail in accordance with the Method of Measurement for this Division.

15.   Testing

Include all necessary labour and materials for testing each part of the system as required during the progress of the work and final testing upon completion. Alternatively testing may be measured under category 15950.

16.   Clean up

Include the cost of cleaning up and disposing rubbish created by the operation of this Division

17.   Electrical wiring and starters

Where the responsibility of this Division, cable, conduit and the like shall be measured in feet; all other work shall be enumerated.

18.   Personnel

Include all managerial, technical and administrative personnel necessary to ensure efficient operation of the contract, together with all attendant expenses.

CLASSIFICATIONS (Continued)

1. 19. Layout

Include all labour, material and instruments required for laying out the work of this Division.

20. Hoisting

Include hoisting major equipment of this Division which is beyond the capabilities of the General Contractor's hoisting equipment.

21. Plant and equipment

Include providing, installing and operating all tools and equipment used by this Division including fuel, maintenance, repairs and spare parts.

22. Site visits

Include the cost of all expenses incurred by supervisory staff on regular visits to the Works.

23. Scaffolding

Shall be enumerated by sections, giving height, and stating if special wheels are required.

24. Premium time

Include any special measures in respect of work involving overtime or shift work.

25. Bonds

Include Bid, Performance, Payment and Guarantee Bonds, Certified Cheques and Securities, stating the amount of the cover and whether payable by the Owner or Contractor.

26. Travel expenses

Include time lost in travel to and from Site and all fares payable under trade agreements and allowances for board and lodging.

CLASSIFICATIONS (Continued)

1.   27.   Lost time

Include time lost in reporting to Site when work is unable to be performed due to inclement weather as stated in Trade Agreement.

28.   Sales taxes and duties

Include all sales taxes and duties in effect at the time of the Tender including any special exemptions or reimbursements.

29.   Cutting, patching and making good

Unless measured in other Divisions, cutting, patching, canning, coring and making good shall be enumerated. The removal and replacement of ceilings and walls for access purposes shall be measured in square feet.

15080 - MECHANICAL INSULATION

1.   Duct, equipment and piping insulation shall be measured in this category.

2.   Piping insulation shall be measured in feet, and the purpose of the pipe stated. An allowance of 1 foot, 6 inches of insulation shall be allowed for each fitting or valve.

3.   Equipment insulation shall be measured in square feet, and the item of equipment stated.

4.   Ductwork insulation shall be measured in square feet.

5.   Prefabricated insulated panels shall be measured in square feet and the number of panels shall be stated.

6.   An insulation media, for use with an underground distribution system, shall be measured in cubic feet, or by weight.

15100 - BUILDING SERVICES PIPING

1. Building services piping shall be measured in the following categories:

    15140 - Domestic water piping
    15150 - Sanitary waste and vent piping
    15160 - Storm drainage piping
    15170 - Swimming pool and fountain piping
    15180 - Heating and cooling piping
    15190 - Fuel piping

2. Valves, pumps, floor drains etc. shall be measured in the category to which they relate.

3. For less complex projects, all mechanical work relating to heating, ventilating and air conditioning may be measured in Category 15180; in this case it would contain items detailed in Sections 15100 - Building Services Piping, 15500 - Heat-generation Equipment, 15600 - Refrigeration Equipment, 15800 - Air Distribution and 15900 - HVAC Instrumentation and Controls.

15200 - PROCESS PIPING

1. Process piping shall be measured in the following categories:

    15210 - Process air and gas piping
    15220 - Process water and waste piping
    15230 - Industrial process piping

15300 - FIRE PROTECTION PIPING

1. Fire protection shall be measured either in this category or in Division 13 Category 13900.

15400 - PLUMBING FIXTURES AND EQUIPMENT

1. Plumbing fixtures and equipment shall be measured in the following categories:

    15410 - Plumbing fixtures
    15440 - Plumbing pumps
    15450 - Potable water storage tanks
    15480 - Domestic water heaters
    15490 - Pool and fountain equipment

15400 - PLUMBING FIXTURES AND EQUIPMENT (Continued)

2.   Plumbing equipment shall include pumps, storage tanks, water heaters, etc.

3.   Special systems shall include compressed air, fuel oil, natural gas, oxygen, vacuum, etc.   Each system shall be measured separately under an appropriate heading.

15500 - HEAT-GENERATION EQUIPMENT

1.   Heat-generation equipment shall be measured in the following categories:

   15510 - Heating boilers and accessories
   15520 - Feedwater equipment
   15530 - Furnaces
   15540 - Fuel-fired heaters
   15550 - Breechings, chimneys and stacks

15600 - REFRIGERATION EQUIPMENT

1.   Refrigeration equipment shall be measured in the following categories:

   15610 - Refrigeration compressors
   15620 - Packaged water chillers
   15640 - Packaged cooling towers
   15650 - Field-erected cooling towers
   15660 - Liquid coolers and evaporative condensers
   15670 - Refrigerant condensing units

15700 - HEATING, VENTILATING AND AIR CONDITIONING EQUIPMENT

1.   Heating, ventilating and air conditioning equipment shall be measured in the following categories:

   15710 - Heat exchangers
   15720 - Air handling units
   15730 - Unitary air conditioning equipment
   15740 - Heat pumps
   15750 - Humidity control equipment
   15760 - Terminal heating and cooling units
   15770 - Floor-heating and snow-melting equipment
   15780 - Energy recovery equipment

15700 - HEATING, VENTILATING AND AIR CONDITIONING EQUIPMENT (Continued)

2. All work within a boiler room, and within an equipment room, shall be so stated, and each shall be kept separate.

3. An item of equipment which is to be assembled on site shall have the number of component parts enumerated.

15800 - AIR DISTRIBUTION

1. Air distribution shall be measured in the following categories:

    15810 - Ducts
    15820 - Duct accessories
    15830 - Fans
    15840 - Air terminal units
    15850 - Air outlets and inlets
    15860 - Air cleaning devices

2. Rectangular and circular ductwork shall be measured in feet and the resultant length converted into weight, as follows:

    1. Measure straight lengths between fittings and round up to next 1 foot above, e.g. 7 feet, 3 inches is rounded up to 8 feet.

    2. Measure transitions to nearest 1 foot and state the greater dimension at each end of the transition.

    3. Measure square elbows as the sum of the two long sides and round off to the nearest 1 foot length; state the cross-sectional dimensions.

    4. Measure radius elbows as the sum of the tangential lengths and round off to the nearest 1 foot length; state the cross-sectional dimensions.

    5. Measure "Y" fittings as the equivalent of two 45° radius elbows.

    6. Measure the length of tap-in tees, registers and diffuser collars and round off to the nearest 1 foot length (minimum length 1 foot); state the cross-sectional dimensions of the larger end.

    7. Measure 45° elbows at the straight length between the two extremes of the elbow and round off to the nearest 1 foot length; state the cross-sectional dimensions.

15800 - AIR DISTRIBUTION (Continued)

2. 8. Measure offsets as the equivalent of two 45° elbows.

9. Measure duct ends as the length of the lesser dimension of the end and round off to the nearest 1 foot.

10. Enumerate the number of fittings in order to calculate the "fitting to duct length" ratio for pricing purposes.

11. To the total weight of duct (the conversion of length to weight shall be obtained from appropriate tables) add the following:

1. Sheet metal ducts - 20% to cover seams, joints, cleats, hangers, sealants and waste.

2. Fibreglass ducts - 15% to cover waste plus 15 pounds per 100 square feet to cover hangers and supports.

3. Duct liners - 15% to cover waste.

4. Welded black iron ducts - 30% to cover seams, joints, cleats, hangers, sealants and waste.

3. Spiral ductwork shall be measured in feet. All fittings shall be enumerated.

4. Prefabricated insulated panels shall be measured in square feet and the number of panels shall be stated. This work may be measured in category 15080.

15900 - HVAC INSTRUMENTATION AND CONTROLS

1.   HVAC instrumentation and controls shall be measured in the following categories:

> 15905 - HVAC instrumentation
> 15910 - Direct digital controls
> 15915 - Electric and electronic controls
> 15920 - Pneumatic controls
> 15925 - Pneumatic and electric controls
> 15930 - Self-powered controls
> 15935 - Building systems controls

15950 - TESTING, ADJUSTING AND BALANCING

1.   Testing, adjusting and balancing, where not included under General Requirements, shall be given as items in this category.

GENERALLY

1. The section "General Rules" is to be read in conjunction with this Division.

2. Cable, wire, ducts, raceways, conduits, etc. shall be measured in feet; bends, fittings, supports, fastenings and all other items in this Division shall be enumerated.

3. Items which are common to various Sections within this Division shall be measured separately with each Section. E.g. Hangers and supports, sleeves, fire stopping, roof flashings.

CLASSIFICATIONS

1. The various classifications within the scope of "General Requirements" for this Division shall be measured and priced as "Items", unless a specific mode of measurement is recommended, in the following categories:

    1. Certificates and fees

        Include charges pertaining to fees, permits and licenses required for electrical permit, Department of Labour, resistance tests and other similar requirements.

    2. Liability and protection

        Include providing for errors, and protection of finishes.

    3. Record drawings

        Include the cost of producing as built drawings, when or where changes have been made from original drawings.

    4. Shop drawings

        Include processing and checking shop drawings.

    5. Operating instructions and maintenance manuals

        Include providing written operating instructions and maintenance manuals. Where required, shall also include the use of labour, fuel, water and other materials.

CLASSIFICATIONS (Continued)

1. 6. Contractor's shop

    Include:

    1. Providing, maintaining and removing all site offices, storage sheds, welfare accommodation and similar buildings, together with furniture, office equipment, services, and including all attendance thereon, heating and air conditioning if required.

    2. Installing and all charges for telephone and facsimile facilities.

    7. Temporary and trial usage

    Include, if part of the system is used on a temporary or trial basis, adjusting, cleaning and other similar requirements upon final completion.

    8. Insurances

    Include all contract and labour insurances, including Public Liability, Unemployment, Workmen's Compensation, Hospital, Vacation, Calamity and Marine.

    9. Guarantee

    Include a guarantee to cover defects in materials and workmanship for a specified period of time.

    10. Identification tags

    Include providing identification tags.

    11. Bases and supports

    Include steel bases or stands for electrical equipment unless specifically measured with the item concerned. Shall also include all miscellaneous steelwork related to this Division including that required for seismic bracing.

    12. Testing

    Include all necessary labour and materials for testing each part of the system as required during the progress of the work and final testing upon completion.

CLASSIFICATIONS (Continued)

1. 13. Clean up

   Include the cost of cleaning up and disposing rubbish created by the operation of this Division.

   14. Personnel

   Include all managerial, technical and administrative personnel necessary to ensure efficient operation of the contract, together with all attendant expenses.

   15. Layout

   Include all labour, material and instruments required for laying out the work of this Division.

   16. Hoisting

   Include hoisting major equipment of this Division which is beyond the capabilities of the General Contractor's hoisting equipment.

   17. Plant and equipment

   Include providing, installing and operating all tools and equipment used by this Division including fuel, maintenance, repairs and spare parts.

   18. Site visits

   Include the cost of all expenses incurred by supervisory staff on regular visits to the Works.

   19. Scaffolding

   Shall be enumerated by sections, giving height, and stating if special wheels are required.

   20. Premium time

   Include any special measures in respect of work involving overtime or shift work.

CLASSIFICATIONS (Continued)

1. 21. Bonds

   Include Bid, Performance, Payment and Guarantee Bonds, Certified Cheques and Securities, stating the amount of the cover and whether payable by the Owner or Contractor.

   22. Travel expenses

   Include time lost in travel to and from the Site and all fares payable under trade agreements and allowances for board and lodging.

   23. Lost time

   Include time lost in reporting to Site when work is unable to be performed due to inclement weather as stated in Trade Agreement.

   24. Sales taxes and duties

   Include all sales taxes and duties in effect at the time of the Tender including any special exemptions or reimbursements.

   25. Cutting, patching and making good

   Unless measured in other Divisions, cutting, patching, canning, coring and making good shall be enumerated. The removal and replacement of ceilings and walls for access purposes shall be measured in square feet.

16100 - WIRING METHODS

1. Wiring etc. shall be measured in the following categories:

   16120 - Conductors and cables
   16130 - Raceways and boxes
   16140 - Wiring devices
   16150 - Wiring connections

16200 - ELECTRICAL POWER

1.   Electrical power shall be measured in the following categories:

> 16210 - Electrical utility services
> 16220 - Motors and generators
> 16230 - Generator assemblies
> 16240 - Battery equipment
> 16260 - Static power converters
> 16270 - Transformers
> 16280 - Power filters and conditioners
> 16290 - Power measurement and control

16300 - TRANSMISSION AND DISTRIBUTION

1.   Transmission and distribution shall be measured in the following categories:

> 16310 - Transmission and distribution accessories
> 16320 - High-voltage switching and protection
> 16330 - Medium-voltage switching and protection
> 16340 - Medium-voltage switching and protection assemblies
> 16360 - Unit substations

16400 - LOW-VOLTAGE DISTRIBUTION

1.   Low-voltage distribution shall be measured in the following categories:

> 16410 - Enclosed switches and circuit breakers
> 16420 - Enclosed controllers
> 16430 - Low-voltage switchgear
> 16440 - Switchboards, panelboards and control centres
> 16450 - Enclosed bus assemblies
> 16460 - Low-voltage transformers
> 16470 - Power distribution units

16500 - LIGHTING

1.   Lighting shall be measured in the following categories:

> 16510 - Interior luminaires
> 16520 - Exterior luminaires
> 16530 - Emergency lighting
> 16550 - Special purpose lighting
> 16570 - Dimming control
> 16580 - Lighting accessories

16700 - COMMUNICATIONS

1.   Communications shall be measured in the following categories:

> 16710 - Communications circuits
> 16720 - Telephone and intercommunication equipment
> 16740 - Communications and data processing equipment
> 16770 - Cable transmission and reception equipment
> 16780 - Broadcast transmission and reception equipment
> 16790 - Microwave transmission and reception equipment,

16800 - SOUND AND VIDEO

1.   Sound and video shall be measured in the following categories:

> 16810 - Sound and video circuits
> 16820 - Sound reinforcement

Method of Measurement of Construction Works

Seventh Edition

Useful Information

International System of Units (SI)

The International System of Units (SI) is based on seven fundamental (base) units:

SI base units

Base quantity	Name	Symbol
length	metre	m
mass	kilogram	kg
time	second	s
electric current	ampere	A
thermodynamic temperature	kelvin	K
amount of substance	mole	mol
luminous intensity	candela	cd

The same name and the same symbol are used to express a temperature interval, and a temperature interval may also be expressed in degrees Celsius, symbol °C. It should also be noted that °C interval = K interval, but 0 °C = 273 K.

There are also a number of derived units which are combinations of base units and which may have special names and symbols:

Examples of SI derived units

Derived quantity	Name	Symbol
area	square metre	m^2
volume	cubic metre	m^3
density, mass density	kilogram per cubic metre	kg/m^3
specific volume	cubic metre per kilogram	m^3/kg
current density	ampere per square metre	A/m^2
magnetic field strength	ampere per metre	A/m
luminance	candela per square metre	cd/m^2

SI Symbols

Symbol	Name	Quantity	Formula
A	ampere	electric current	base unit
Bq	becquerel	activity (of a radio nuclide)	1/s
C	coulomb	electric charge	A·s
°C	degree Celsius	temperature interval	°C = K *
cd	candela	luminous intensity	base unit
F	farad	electric capacitance	C/V
Gy	gray	absorbed dose	J/kg
g	gram	mass	kg/1000
H	henry	inductance	Wb/A
Hz	hertz	frequency	1/s
ha	hectare	area	10,000 m^2
J	joule	energy, work, heat	N·m
K	kelvin	temperature	base unit
kg	kilogram	mass	base unit
L	litre	volume	m^3/1000
lm	lumen	luminous flux	cd·sr
lx	lux	illuminance	lm/m^2
m	metre	length	base unit
mol	mole	amount of substance	base unit
N	newton	force	kg·m/s^2
Ω	ohm	electric resistance	V/A
Pa	pascal	pressure, stress	N/m^2
rad	radian	plane angle	m/m (dimensionless)
S	siemens	electric conductance	A/V
s	second	time	base unit
sr	steradian	solid angle	m^2/m^2 (dimensionless)
T	tesla	magnetic flux density	Wb/m^2
t	tonne, metric ton	mass	1000 kg; Mg
V	volt	electric potential	W/A
W	watt	power, radiant flux	J/s
Wb	weber	magnetic flux	V·s

See note under SI Base Units on prior page with regard to use of °C and K.

Use of Symbols

The correct use of symbols is important because an incorrect symbol may change the meaning of a quantity.

- SI has no abbreviations - only symbols. Therefore, no periods follow a symbol except at the end of a sentence.

    Examples: A, *not* amp; s, *not* sec; SI *not* S.I.

- Symbols appear in lower case unless the unit name has been taken from a proper name. In this case the first letter of the symbol is capitalized.

    Examples: m, metre; Pa, pascal; W, watt
    Exception: L, litre

- Symbols and prefixes are printed in upright (roman) type regardless of the type style in surrounding text.

    Example: *...a distance of* 73 km *between ...*

- Unit symbols are the same whether singular or plural.

    Examples: 1 mm, 100 mm; 1 kg, 65 kg

- Leave a space between the value and the symbol.

    Examples: 115 W, *not* 115W; 0.75 L, *not* 0.75L; 88 °C, *not* 88°C or 88° C
    Exception: No space is left between the numerical value and symbol for degree of plane angle, e.g., 73°, not 73 °

- Note: Symbol for coulomb is C; for degree Celsius it is °C.

- Do not mix symbols and names in the same expression.

    Examples: radians per second or rad/s not radians/second; not radians/s
    m/s or metres per second; not metres/second; not metres/s
    J/kg or joules per kilogram; not joules/kilogram; not joules/kg

- Symbol for product - use the raised dot ($\cdot$)

    Examples: N·m; mPa·s; W/(m^2·K)

Use of Symbols (continued)

- Symbol for quotient - use one of the following forms:

    Example: m/s or $\frac{m}{s}$ or use negative exponent

- Note: Use only one solidus (/) per expression and parentheses to avoid any ambiguity.

Multiples and Submultiples

SI units make use of a series of prefixes and prefix symbols to indicate orders of magnitude in steps of 1 000 and provide a convenient way to express large and small numbers and to eliminate nonsignificant digits and leading zeros in decimal fractions.

Multiplying factor	Prefix	Symbol	Multiplying factor	Prefix	Symbol
$1\ 000\ 000\ 000\ 000 = 10^{12}$	tera	T	$0.1 = 10^{-1}$	deci	d
$1\ 000\ 000\ 000 = 10^{9}$	giga	G	$0.01 = 10^{-2}$	centi	c
$1\ 000\ 000 = 10^{6}$	mega	M	$0.001 = 10^{-3}$	milli	m
$1\ 000 = 10^{3}$	kilo	k	$0.000\ 001 = 10^{-6}$	micro	μ
$100 = 10^{2}$	hecto	h	$0.000\ 000\ 001 = 10^{-9}$	nano	n
$10 = 10^{1}$	deca	da	$0.000\ 000\ 000\ 001 = 10^{-12}$	pico	p

Examples: 64 000 watts is the same as 64 kilowatts*
0.057 metres is the same as 57 millimetres
16 000 metres is the same as 16 kilometres*.
* except for intended accuracy

Other prefixes adopted for use with SI units are noted below.

Multiplying factor	Prefix	Symbol	Multiplying factor	Prefix	Symbol
10^{24}	yotta	Y	10^{-15}	femto	f
10^{21}	zetta	Z	10^{-18}	atto	a
10^{18}	exa	E	10^{-21}	zepto	z
10^{15}	peta	P	10^{-24}	yocto	y

Multiples and Submultiples (continued)

To realize the full benefit of the prefixes when expressing a quantity by numerical value, choose a prefix so that the number lies between 0.1 and 1 000. For simplicity, give preference to prefixes representing 1 000 raised to an integral power (i.e. μm, mm, km).

> *Exceptions:* In expressing area and volume, the prefixes hecto, deka, deci, and centi may be required; for example, cubic decimetre (L), square hectometre (hectare), cubic centimetre.

Tables of values of the same quantity.

- Comparison of values.
  For certain quantities in particular applications. For example, the millimetre is used for linear dimensions in architectural and engineering drawings even when the values lie far outside the range of 0.1 mm to 1 000 mm; the centimetre is usually used for anatomical measurements and clothing sizes.

- Compound units.
  A compound unit is a derived unit expressed with two or more units. The prefix is attached to a unit in the numerator.

  > *Exception:* V/m *not* mV/mm
  > MJ/kg *not* kJ/g

- Compound prefixes.
  Prefixes formed by a combination of two or more prefixes are not used. Use only one prefix.

  > *Examples:* 2 nm *not* 2 mμm
  > 6 m^3 *not* 6 kL
  > 6 MPa *not* 6 kkPa

- Exponential Powers.
  An exponent attached to a symbol containing a prefix indicates that the multiple (of the unit with its prefix) is raised to the power of 10 expressed by the exponent.

  > *Examples:* $1 \text{ mm}^3 = (10^{-3}\text{m})^3 = 10^{-9}\text{m}^3$
  > $1 \text{ ns}^{-1} = (10^{-9}\text{s})^{-1} = 10^{-9}\text{s}^{-1}$
  > $1 \text{ mm}^2/\text{s} = (10^{-3}\text{m})^2/\text{s} = 10^{-6}\text{m}^2/\text{s}$

Numbers

SI principles state that in writing numbers, the dot (.) or the comma (,) is used only to separate the whole part of a number from the decimal part. Numbers may be divided in groups of three in order to facilitate reading; neither dots nor commas are ever inserted in the spaces between groups. In numbers of four digits, the space is not necessary except for uniformity in tables.

> *Examples:* 6.358 568; 85 365; 51 845 953; 88 000; 0.246 113 562; 7 258

Small numbers. When writing numbers less than one, always put a zero before the decimal marker.

> *Example:* 0.046

Because billion means a million million in most countries but a thousand million in the United States, avoid using billion in technical writing.

Do's and Don'ts

- The units in the international system of units are called SI units - not Metric Units and not SI Metric Units.

- Non-SI units in the US are called Inch-Pound units (I-P units) - not conventional units, not US customary units, not English units, and not Imperial units.

- Treat all spelled out names as nouns. Therefore, do not capitalize the first letter of a unit except at the beginning of a sentence or in capitalized material such as a title.

  > *Examples:*   watt; pascal; ampere; volt; newton; kelvin
  > *Exception:*   Always capitalize the first letter of Celsius.

- Do not begin a sentence with a unit symbol - either rearrange the words or write the unit name in full.

- Use plurals for spelled out words when required by the rules of grammar.

  > *Examples:* metre - metres; henry - henries; kilogram - kilograms; kelvin – kelvins
  > *Exceptions:* hertz - hertz; lux - lux; siemens - siemens

- Do not put a space or hyphen between the prefix and unit name.

  > *Examples:*   kilometer; not kilo metre; not kilo-metre;
  >   milliwatt; not milli watt; not milli-watt.

Do's and Don'ts (continued)

- When a prefix ends with a vowel and the unit name begins with a vowel, retain and pronounce both vowels.

  Example: kiloampere
  Exceptions: hectare; kilohm; megohm

- When compound units are formed by multiplication, leave a space between units that are multiplied.

  Examples: newton metre; not newton-metre
                   volt ampere; not volt-ampere.

- Use the modifier squared or cubed after the unit name.

  Example: metre per second squared

  Exception: For area or volume the modifier may be placed before the units.
  Example: square millimetre; cubic metre

- When compound units are formed by division, use the word *per*, not a solidus (/).

  Examples: metre per second; not metre/second;
                   watt per square metre; not watt/square metre.

- Do not use modifying terms such as electrical, alternating current, etc., after the symbol.

  Examples: kPa (gage); MW (e); V (ac).

Calculation of Areas

Parallelogram - a quadrilateral with parallel opposite sides

Area $= b \times h$

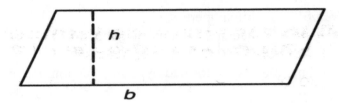

Trapezoid - a quadrilateral having two, and only two, parallel sides

Area $= h \times \frac{1}{2} (b + c)$

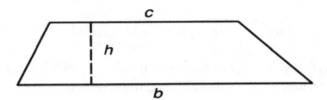

Triangle - a three-sided polygon

Area $= \frac{1}{2} (b \times h)$

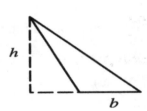 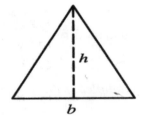

Irregular Polygons

The areas of irregular polygons can be determined by dividing the areas into the shapes as shown below and adding the areas of the parts

Area $= \frac{1}{2} (a \times b) + (c \times \frac{1}{2} (b + d)) + \frac{1}{2} (e \times d)$

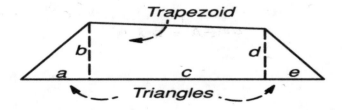

Calculation of Areas (continued)

Circle

C = Circumference
D = Diameter
R = Radius

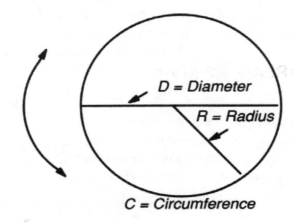

Area	$= D^2 \times 0.785\,4$
	$= R^2 \times 3.141\,6$
	$= C^2 \times 0.079\,58$
Diameter	$= R \times 2$
	$= C \times 0.318\,31$
Circumference	$= D \times 3.141\,6$
	$= R \times 3.141\,6 \times 2$
Radius	$= D \div 2$
	$= C \times 0.159\,155$

Other Formulae

Surface of sphere $= 4 \times 3.141\,6 \times R^2$
Volume of sphere $= {}^4/_3 \times 3.141\,6 \times R^3$
Volume of pyramid or cone $= {}^1/_3$ base area x height

Conversions - Imperial to SI

Length / Linear Measure

From	To	Multiply by
inches	millimetres	25.400 0
inches	metres	0.025 4
feet	metres	0.304 8
yards	metres	0.914 4
miles	kilometres	1.609 3

Area

From	To	Multiply by
square feet	square metres (m^2)	0.092 9
square yards	square metres (m^2)	0.836 1
square miles	square kilometres (km^2)	2.589 9
acres	hectares (ha)	0.404 7

1 square foot	=	144 square inches
1 square yard	=	9 square feet
1 square	=	100 square feet
1 acre	=	43,560 square feet
1 square mile	=	640 acres

Volume

From	To	Multiply by
cubic feet	cubic metres (m^3)	0.028 3
cubic yards	cubic metres (m^3)	0.764 6
Imperial gallons	litres	4.546 0
US gallons	litres	3.785 3

1 cubic foot	=	6.24 imperial gallons
1 cubic yard	=	27 cubic feet
1 imperial gallon	=	1.201 US gallons

Weight

From	To	Multiply by
pounds	kilograms (kg)	0.453 6
short ton	kilograms (kg)	907.185 0
long ton	kilograms (kg)	1016.050 0
short ton	tonne (t)	0.907 2
long ton	tonne (t)	1.016 0

1 short ton	=	2,000 pounds
1 long ton	=	2,240 pounds

Conversions - SI to Imperial

Length / Linear Measure

From	To	Multiply by
millimetres	inches	0.039 4
metres	inches	39.369 6
metres	feet	3.280 8
metres	yards	1.093 6
kilometres	miles	0.621 4

1 metre	=	1 000 mm
1 kilometre	=	1 000 metres

Area

From	To	Multiply by
square metres (m^2)	square feet	10.763 9
square metres (m^2)	square yards	1.195 9
square kilometres (km^2)	square miles	0.386 1
hectares	acres	2.471 0

1 square metre (m^2)	=	10 000.00 square centimetres
1 hectares (ha)	=	10 000.00 square metres (m^2)
1 square kilometre (km^2)	=	100 hectares (ha)

Volume

From	To	Multiply by
cubic metres (m^3)	cubic feet	35.314 7
cubic metres (m^3)	cubic yards	1.307 9
litres	imperial gallons	0.219 9
litres	US gallons	0.264 2

1 cubic metre (m^3)	=	1 000 litres (L)

Weight

From	To	Multiply by
kilograms (kg)	pounds	2.204 6
kilograms (kg)	short ton	0.001 102
kilograms (kg)	long ton	0.000 984

1 tonne (t)	=	1 000 kilograms (kg)

Reinforcing Steel - Comparison of Imperial and Metric Sizes

Imperial Bar			Metric Bar			Metric Bar is	
Bar Size	Area in^2	Area mm^2	Bar Size	Area in^2	Area mm^2		
# 3	0.11	71	10M	0.16	100	45.0%	L
# 4	0.20	129	10M	0.16	100	20.0%	S
# 4	0.20	129	15M	0.31	200	55.0%	L
# 5	0.31	200	15M	0.31	200	Same	
# 6	0.44	284	20M	0.47	300	6.8%	L
# 7	0.60	387	20M	0.47	300	22.0%	S
# 7	0.60	387	25M	0.78	500	30.0%	L
# 8	0.79	510	25M	0.78	500	1.3%	S
# 9	1.00	645	30M	1.09	700	9.0%	L
# 10	1.27	819	30M	1.09	700	14.0%	S
# 10	1.27	819	35M	1.55	1 000	22.0%	L
# 11	1.56	1 006	35M	1.55	1 000	0.6%	S
#14	2.25	1 452	45M	2.33	1 500	3.5%	L
#18	4.00	2 581	55M	3.88	2 500	3.0%	S

L = Larger   S = Smaller

Reinforcing Steel - Weights

Imperial Bar	
Bar Size	Weight pounds / foot
# 3	0.375
# 4	0.668
# 5	1.043
# 6	1.502
# 7	2.044
# 8	2.670
# 9	3.400
# 10	4.303
# 11	5.313
# 14	7.650
# 16	10.413
# 18	13.600

Metric Bar		
Bar Size	Mass kg/m	Diameter mm
10M	0.785	11.3
15M	1.570	16.0
20M	2.355	19.5
25M	3.925	25.2
30M	5.495	29.9
35M	7.850	35.7
45M	11.775	43.7
55M	19.625	56.4

Contact us

Canadian Institute of Quantity Surveyors
P.O. Box 124, STN R
Toronto ON M4G 3Z3
Tel: (905) 471-0882   Fax: (905) 471-7545

E-mail: info@ciqs.org
Web site: www.ciqs.org

Affiliated Associations

Newfoundland and Labrador Association of Quantity Surveyors (NLAQS)
Box 14, 208 Hussey Drive
St. John's NF A1A 4Z5
Tel: (709) 722-0505   Fax: (709) 722-1504

E-mail: nlaqs@ciqs.org

Nova Scotia Association of Quantity Surveyors (NSAQS)
P.O. Box 8774, STN A
Halifax NS B3K 5M4

E-mail: nsaqs@ciqs.org
Web site: www.ciqs.org/nsaqs/

Les Économistes en Construction du Québec / Quantity Surveyors of Quebec (QSQ)
c/o Association de la Construction du Québec
7400, boul. des Galeries d'Anjou, suite 205
Anjou QC H1M 3M2
Tel: (514) 354-3857   Fax (514) 354-6480

E-mail: qsq@ciqs.org
Web site: www.ecq-qsq.org/

Ontario Institute of Quantity Surveyors (OIQS)
P.O. Box 124, STN R
Toronto ON M4G 3Z3
Tel: (905) 471-0882   Fax: (905) 471-7545

E-mail: info@oiqs.org
Web site: www.oiqs.org

Association of Quantity Surveyors of Alberta (AQSA)
P.O. Box 57051 SPO 2525 - 36th St. N.E.
Calgary AB T1Y 6R4
Tel: (403) 252-7070   Fax: (403) 291-0983

E-mail: aqsa@ciqs.org
Web site: www.qs-alta.org

Quantity Surveyors Society of British Columbia (QSSBC)
1519 – 8th Avenue
New Westminster BC V3M 2S5
Tel: (604) 521-3671   Fax: (604) 521-6632

E-mail: info@qssbc.org
Web site: www.qssbc.org

Publications

The following publications are produced by the Canadian Institute of Quantity Surveyors. For ordering information, contact the Canadian Institute of Quantity Surveyors at (905) 471-0882 or order on-line at www.ciqs.org.

Method of Measurement of Construction Works,
7th edition, 2000. ISBN # 1-896606-28-8

Elemental Cost Analysis, Measurement of Buildings by Area & Volume
3rd edition, 2000. ISBN # 1-896606-30-X

Construction Budgeting
2nd edition, 1998. ISBN # 1-896606-26-1

Canadian Building Law
5th edition, 2001. ISBN # 1-896606-34-2

Construction Planning & Scheduling - An Introduction
1st edition, 1997. ISBN # 1-896606-16-4

Available Services & Finding, Selecting and Engaging a Quantity Surveyor
1st edition, 2002. ISBN # 1-896606-36-9

Quantity Surveying & Cost Consulting Services
Schedule of Services and Recommended Charges
4th edition, 2002. ISBN # 1-896606-38-5

Careers in the Value Professions, Quantity Surveying and Construction Estimating
1997. ISBN # 1-896606-18-0

Construction Economist (quarterly journal of the CIQS)
ISBN #0836-6179

Index of Standard Abbreviations
2nd edition, 1994.

Estimate Pads (take-off paper)